ANDOVER PAST

First published 2001
by Historical Publications Ltd
32 Ellington Street, London N7 8PL
(Tel: 020-7607 1628)

ISBN 0948667 74 5
British Library Cataloguing-in-Data
A catalogue record for this book is available from the British Library

Typeset in Palatino by Historical Publications
Reproduction by G & J Graphics, London EC2
Printed by Edelvives in Zaragoza, Spain

The Illustrations

The following have kindly given their consent to reproduction of illustrations:
Bath Postal Museum *63*
Dacre family *7*
Hubert Earney *85, 106, 117, 129, 131, 133, 134, 135, 136, 138, 139, 141, 143, 147*
Hampshire County Museums Service *42, 45, 46, 79*
Hampshire County Record Office *41*
John D.G. Isherwood *148*
Linnean Society *73*
Queen's College, Oxford *32*
Anthony C. Raper *1, 2, 17, 18, 19, 24, 33, 36, 37, 38, 39, 40, 43, 47, 52, 56, 57, 60, 64, 65, 68, 71, 72, 74, 76, 80, 84, 89, 90, 91, 92, 93, 94, 96, 97, 101, 102, 103, 104, 105, 107, 108, 109, 110, 118, 119, 122, 124, 125, 128, 137, 140, 144, 149, 153*
Royal Commission for Historical Monuments *9*
Derek Tempero *57, 75, 87, 99, 114, 115, 116, 130, 132, 142, 145*
Test Valley Borough Council *151, 152*
Richard Warmington *23*

ANDOVER PAST

Anthony C. Raper

HISTORICAL PUBLICATIONS

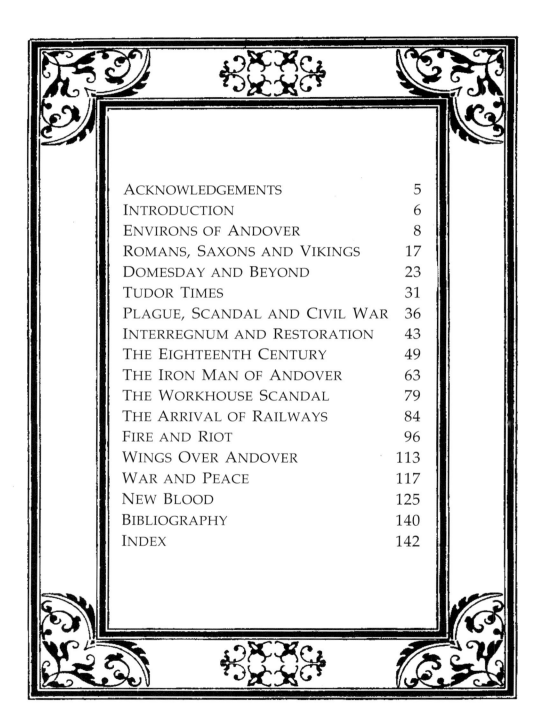

ACKNOWLEDGEMENTS	5
INTRODUCTION	6
ENVIRONS OF ANDOVER	8
ROMANS, SAXONS AND VIKINGS	17
DOMESDAY AND BEYOND	23
TUDOR TIMES	31
PLAGUE, SCANDAL AND CIVIL WAR	36
INTERREGNUM AND RESTORATION	43
THE EIGHTEENTH CENTURY	49
THE IRON MAN OF ANDOVER	63
THE WORKHOUSE SCANDAL	79
THE ARRIVAL OF RAILWAYS	84
FIRE AND RIOT	96
WINGS OVER ANDOVER	113
WAR AND PEACE	117
NEW BLOOD	125
BIBLIOGRAPHY	140
INDEX	142

Acknowledgements

During the writing of this book two very special friends have passed away. Both were persons whom I admired greatly for their knowledge and expertise in their subject.

George Brickell, whose interest in local history stretches back before the last war, was a great local historian and author of many articles and monographs on aspects of Andover's history. His enthusiasm for his subject first encouraged me to take up local history research and to publish my findings.

Max Dacre, chairman of the Andover Archaeological Society, a good friend and a great character, he was undoubtedly the town's greatest archaeologist. Max and his wife Peggy were the first friends my wife and I made when moving into the town. He was a very professional amateur and his views and work were respected and admired by many of the country's eminent archaeologists. Max guided me through the maze of Andover's early pre-history vetting the first few chapters of this book, and made many useful suggestions as to what should be included or deleted.

Thanks must also go to Dave Allen, Curator of Andover Museum and the Hampshire County Museum Service's Keeper of Archaeology, for his support. He also looked over my archaeological notes and provided a number of illustrations for the book. I am grateful also to Frank Green, former Field Director of the Test Valley Archaeological Trust, who checked my notes relating to their area of interest and allowed me to view their records.

I am indebted to my good friend and fellow historian, Derek Tempero, a past editor of the *Andover Advertiser* newspaper, for his encouragement to get me to complete this book and for the loan of a number of the pictures in this book. There are more I should mention for their help with information and illustrations, but the list would be long and tedious. To all those who helped I am very grateful, but a special thankyou is due to Bert Earney, John Isherwood and Harry Paris. I also give thanks and praise to my friends and colleagues in the Andover Local History and Archaeology Society for their tireless effort in promoting the history of our town.

Andover is not my birth town. I am one of the London overspill, or so we were called in the 60s and 70s, but I adopted Andover and, as I've lived here 28 years, I consider it my town now. This book is dedicated to all the past historians and archaeologists who did everything they could to bring their findings to the people of Andover and district.

A.C.R. 2001

Introduction

The town of Andover, Hampshire lies in a natural bowl formed at the head of the rivers Test and Anton at the edge of the great forests of Chute and Harewood. Winchester, once the Saxon capital of England, lies 14 miles distant in a south-easterly direction, and the city of Salisbury just 18 miles south-west of Andover across the Wiltshire border. In a northerly direction, just over the Berkshire border, is the small market town of Newbury, while the busy port of Southampton lies just 25 miles to the south.

Andover has for many years been on the main routes from London to the West Country and this remains true today. Access by rail is excellent, Andover being on the main line from Waterloo to Exeter. The town is now bypassed by the A303, which links with the M3 some ten miles to the east, bringing London (66 miles) and the south coast (approx. 25 miles) within easy reach. Thruxton, six miles to the west, is the nearest operational airfield, used by light fixed-wing planes and helicopters.

Andover today is very different from fifty years ago, for then it was but a small market town with a population of around 5,000. It supported then an agricultural community and life there reflected their values. But Andover today, having been designated an 'expanding town' in the 1960s, by Hampshire County Council and the Greater London Council, has developed into a thriving community of around 39,570 with light industry taking over from the slowly declining farming economy.

Nikolaus Pevsner in his book *The Buildings of England – Hampshire and the Isle of Wight* describes Andover in 1967 rather harshly by stating:

> The architectural interest of Andover is very limited – limited to two buildings, indeed. The Greater London Council plan increasing its size from the present 16,000 to 48,000 and of building a completely new centre ought to give Andover precisely what it is lacking.

The only two buildings he considered of interest were the church of St Mary's (completed in 1844) of which he says "The exterior is impressive enough, the interior is sensational", and the 'Grecian style' Guildhall (completed in 1825), with its Doric columns.

He was obviously unimpressed with Andover's architectural heritage. He missed much however, including the 15th-century Angel Inn. Granted the High Street entrance hides its origins behind a 19th-century façade, but take a trip through its carriage arch and see the two-storey timber framing, saved from destruction when the Chantry Way development was begun. Take a look also at the more recently resurrected 15th-century timber framed buildings at the corner of Newbury Street and the Upper High Street and currently used as a hairdressing salon. Both the Angel and the Newbury Street building have somehow survived Town Development and show what Andover would have looked like in the late 15th/16th century.

Perhaps in future years Andover's latest additions to the skyline, the multi-storey car park, Hambledon House and the new Beech Hurst, headquarters of Test Valley Borough Council will fare better in an architect's appraisal of the town.

In fact, Andover is little different to any of the inland Hampshire towns: it never had the wealth of Portsmouth and Southampton, it was not as important as Winchester, the one time capital of England; but it does have a rich history and was an important trading centre and stop-over on the coaching routes to the West Country. This book I hope will do justice to the town of Andover, its history and its inhabitants.

Anthony C. Raper, 2001

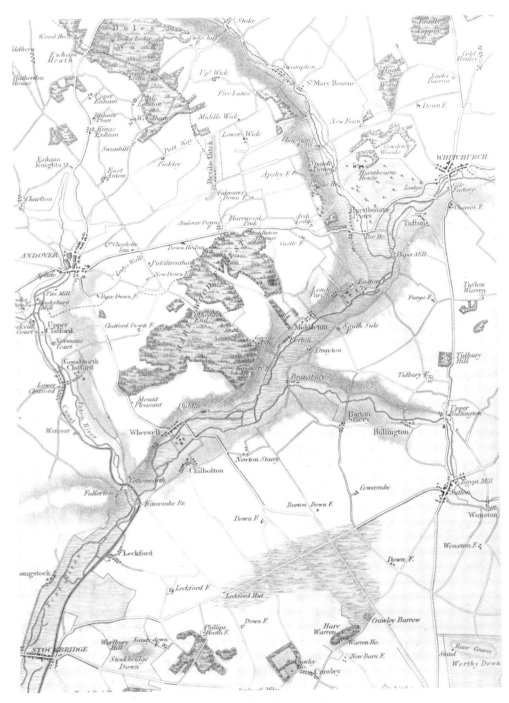

1. *Andover and surrounding countryside c.1835. Map by I. Dower.*

2. *Andover from Bere Hill prior to 1825. Drawn by G.S. Shepherd for Moody's Hampshire, vol. I.*

Environs of Andover

THE CHALK UPLANDS

The greater part of the Andover district consists of chalk uplands, which are an extension of the Salisbury Plain. From this great central mass running eastward are two spurs; the one coming in north of Andover by Kingsclere and Basingstoke, going on to form the North Downs of Surrey and Kent; the other keeping south of Andover, forming the high grounds around Stockbridge, stretching across to Winchester and on, south of Petersfield to the South Downs of Sussex.

The chalk uplands of Southern England were formed between 100 and 65 million years ago during the period which geologists call the Upper Cretaceous Period, when much of north-west Europe lay beneath the sea. Over the years a white chalky mud accumulated on the sea floor composed of the remains of minute sea creatures which abounded in the shallow sea. Great deposits of flint also accumulated, often in layers, in the chalk seabed. The flint is a silica material formed from the skeletons of sponges and marine animals, which survived in the same sea.

On the surrounding land a sub-tropical climate is believed to have existed and the rivers running off deposited clays and sands over the top of the chalk. The weight of these sediments compacted mud into a solid chalk. Later earth movements forced this seabed upward above sea level to form the central ridges of Hampshire, the chalk thrown into folds with tertiary sands and clays in the troughs between. Erosion and the rivers carving their way through the highlands formed the valleys shaping the Hampshire we know today.

Major changes in the climate followed the formation of the new landmasses with two periods of intense cold and glaciation. Hampshire was never covered by ice, for the ice cap did not descend south of the River Thames. All plant life was however destroyed and the flora and fauna of today is the result of the slow creeping back of different species during the later temperate periods.

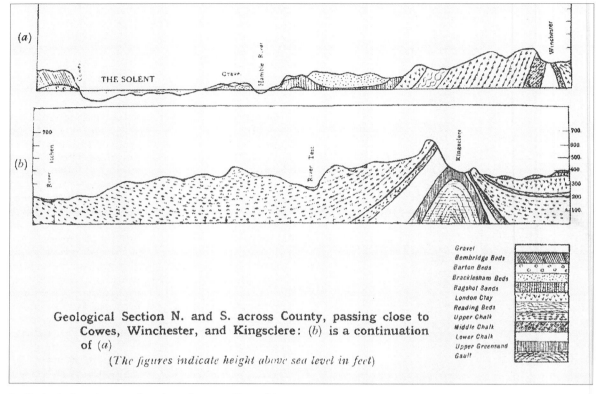

Geological **Section N. and S. across County, passing close to Cowes, Winchester, and Kingsclere**: (*b*) **is a continuation of** (*a*)

(*The figures indicate height above sea level in feet*)

Gravel
Bembridge Beds
Barton Beds
Bracklesham Beds
Bagshot Sands
London Clay
Reading Beds
Upper Chalk
Middle Chalk
Lower Chalk
Upper Greensand
Gault

3. *Geological section, north and south across Hampshire.*

PALEOLITHIC

It was during one of the temperate Palaeolithic periods (*c*.300000 to 12000BC) that man first appeared on the scene in Hampshire. By then most of the area was covered by a dense forest and the high land was bare and inhospitable. Herds of mammoth, elk and woolly rhinoceros roamed the area and man, the hunter, followed in search of food. He left behind tools – crudely fashioned hand axes and scrapers fashioned from the flint so abundant locally.

No evidence exists to show permanent settlement at this time. Flint tools and implements have been found at Hurstbourne in the upper reaches of the Test; Chilbolton on the slopes of West Down; at Shipton Bellinger and in lower reaches of the River Test near Romsey. A mammoth's tooth was also found amongst several worked flints at Hurstbourne.

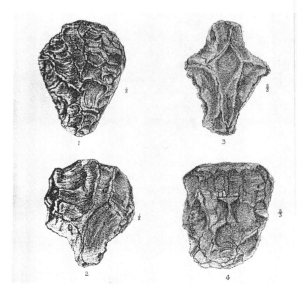

4. *Paleolithic stone tools (taken from 'A Parochial History of St Mary Bourne' by J. Stevens, 1888).*

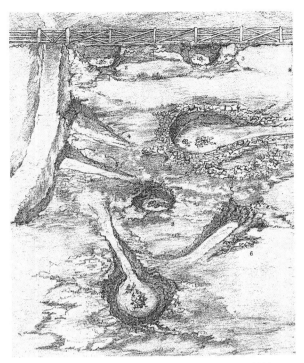

5. Diagram of the pit dwellings at Hurstbourne Sidings (taken from 'A Parochial History of St Mary Bourne', by J. Stevens, 1888).

MESOLITHIC

Climatic changes led to different hunting conditions and a tendency to settle in the Mesolithic period (*c*.12000-4000BC). From this we have numerous finds of flint implements, some of which were made at Norman Court Farm, Upper Clatford.

At Hurstbourne Tarrant near Andover, several pit dwellings of the Mesolithic period were found in 1868 during excavations for a yard adjacent to Hurstbourne Siding, a station on the London & South Western Railway. Just a little way down the Test valley at Braishfield, Mike O'Malley has excavated what is one of the oldest known dwellings in England and near to 100,000 worked flints were found on the site. Mesolithic flint flakes have recently been found in river gravels at a site in Chantry Street, Andover.

NEOLITHIC

The Neolithic period or New Stone Age (*c*.4000 - 2000BC) brought great changes in the behaviour of man. The hunter gradually gave way to the farmer and a far more settled way of life. These people brought with them herds of cattle, sheep and pigs and sowed wheat on the land they had cleared with their stone tools. They were more sophisticated people who had learnt to polish their stone axes and tools to get longer life from them. Further evidence of this is shown by ritual burial of their dead in earthen long barrows and of their use of vessels made from a crude pottery.

Evidence of their existence in the Andover area comes from the excavation of a Long Barrow at Nutbane, by Faith de Morgan in the 1960s. Dr Geoffrey Wainwright discovered Neolithic remains in the form of a number of flints and a hearth at Balksbury, Andover. Other finds have included a polished flint adze at Shepherds Spring to the north of the town; a stone mace-head from Charlton; stone implements from Kimmer Farm at Faccombe; fragments of a polished axe from Quarley with many smaller finds around the town. In addition to the Long Barrow at Nutbane there are four in the Chilbolton area and another at Wallop and several in the Danebury area.

During the latter part of the Neolithic period, around 2400BC, the rite of collective burial petered out as a new wave of immigrants from Europe preferred to bury their dead singly. These people have been called Beaker folk because of their practice of burying a small pottery vessel, which often contained a ritual offering, beside the corpse. The deceased would be laid in a crouching or sleeping position either in a chalk-cut grave (or wooden sided mortuary chamber) or beneath a small round barrow.

THE BRONZE AGE

It appears that there was a large concentration of the Beaker folk in the Wessex area which gradually asserted its influence over a wider area. They brought with them a new culture. A most important development was the appearance of the first weapons and tools made from metal (copper and bronze) along with a fine decorated pottery, the Beaker. A new kind of flint arrowhead appears, known as 'barbed and tanged' along with stone wrist guards and new weapons fashioned from metal (copper and bronze daggers), designed to enhance the prestige and standing of an individual.

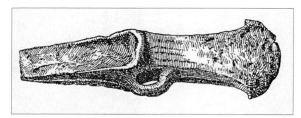

6. *A Bronze Age axehead.*

One of the most important of these Beaker burials came to light in 1986 when the Test Valley Archaeological Trust was asked to provide a watching brief in advance of oil exploration by AMOCO UK. It was located in an area rich in ancient sites on land owned by the John Lewis Partnership on their Leckford estate. From the discoloration of the soil in the general area the burial site appears to have been a round barrow, rather small at five metres diameter, and which over the years has been ploughed away. The grave pit or decayed timber chamber contained two adult males of which the later burial had disturbed the first.

The later burial was of a man aged between 35 and 45, about 5ft 7in tall, average for a man of that time, and accompanying him was a Finger Nail Beaker, containing flint flakes and a flint knife. The primary burial was of a man in his late 20s about 5ft 10in tall and next to him was a Bell Beaker. This contained a copper dagger, an antler spatula, numerous flints, minute stone beads, a gold bead and two sets of gold earrings, making it the richest and earliest example of a Beaker interment in the British Isles. It suggests a man of some importance in the Beaker community, possibly a chieftain.

Further evidence shows that the copper dagger, of which less than a dozen are known, was made from ore found only in the Spanish province of Sevilla. The gold earrings and bead were most likely made from Irish gold and were decorated by a stylus with a slightly rounded point.

THE HARROW WAY

The men of the New Stone Age traded their produce and wares over quite large distances and during this period trading routes and trackways were built up, enabling communities to move about more freely. These were built mainly on the high ground, avoiding the woodland, and curved around the head of streams wherever

possible. The Harrow Way enters the Andover district not far from Quarley Hill, goes around the head of a small stream at Fyfield and takes the ridge by Weyhill to cross the headwaters of the River Anton at Shepherds Spring. From here it runs through the gap between Harewood Forest and Doles Wood, crosses the Bourne rivulet at Chapmansford and ascends the high ground of the Test valley west of Whitchurch. This road must surely be one of the oldest trunk roads in the country, running from the hills just above Penzance in Cornwall to the North Downs above Dover in Kent.

Tin was mined in Devon and Cornwall and may well have been brought along the Harrow Way as far as Weyhill and Andover before being taken to the coastal area near Southampton for transportation to the continent. We know that the Venetian merchants from Southampton traded tin as late as the 15th century. The addition of tin to copper was an important ingredient in the manufacture of bronze, giving it the required degree of hardness for axes and knives etc.

The Neolithic period is the age of henge monuments, used probably for religious purposes, and of causewayed enclosures that may well have been used for feasting and rejoicing. Stonehenge, begun during the early Neolithic period, is without doubt the best known of all the henges and lies about 15 miles west of Andover. Other henges of the later period were constructed at Woodhenge and Durrington Walls. No henge sites have presently come to light within the Test valley. Flint occurs naturally in the chalk beds, sometimes several feet thick and Stone Age man was not averse to mining to obtain it. A great number of such mines exist on the downs at Porton and at Kimpton.

The Neolithic Period merged into the Bronze Age (*c*.2000 to 600BC). Round barrows were a common feature of the landscape and are numerous in the Andover district. There are examples at Weyhill, Penton Mewsey, Portway Industrial Estate, Finkley Down, Walworth Industrial Estate, Tinkers Hill (Picket Piece), and Bere Hill; in fact almost every parish in the area can boast at least one.

A good example of a Bronze Age cremation urn was found when council houses were being built on a field known as 'Dances Land'. A large hoard of bronze weapons including leaf shaped rapiers, large winged spearheads, long ferrules and chapes were found in watercress beds at Shepherds Spring in 1913. They may have been the hoard of a

7. Max and Peggy Dacre. Max was chairman of the Andover Archaeological Society during the late 1960s through to the early 1980s.

bronze founder as many were in an unfinished condition.

During construction of Andover Aerodrome in the early years of this century, at Hundred Acres Field, a Bronze Age round barrow was destroyed. Dr Williams Freeman, then local secretary of the Hampshire Archaeological Society, superintended its removal and from the barrow were retrieved two earthenware vessels, fragments of pottery and burnt broken bones, and a part of a bronze dagger.

Other finds in the area include a looped and socketed spearhead from Grateley, a palstave from the fairground site at Weyhill, two looped palstaves from Vernham's Dean, suggesting fairly large communities residing in the area which were obviously warlike judging from the number of weapon finds.

At Kimpton, five miles west of Andover, a Neolithic and Bronze Age cemetery, in use for 1500 years, was found by the Andover Archaeological Society under the direction of Max Dacre. Finds from the cremated ashes and the urns indicate that a new culture had entered the area, which archaeologists used to describe as Deverel-Rimbury, after two such cemeteries excavated

earlier. These immigrants probably came from the central area of Europe near the Rhine. Their cremations were sometimes placed in urns, at other times not and with practically no grave-goods, but more often they were covered by a slab of pottery or a flint mound and grouped in hundreds. The Kimpton cemetery is considered of national importance and the finds have been accepted by the British Museum for a special display on prehistoric cultures.

THE IRON AGE

Waves of migrants and invaders came across the Channel from north-western France. Celtic speaking, they settled at first on the coast at Hengistbury Head at the mouth of the Hampshire Avon and gradually moved inland. These were a more barbarous race of people, who lived communally, protecting themselves by building hilltop forts. They brought with them the use of iron to make tools and the trading of weapons as currency.

In common with the Deverel-Rimbury and earlier cultures, these Iron Age people were farmers and mixed easily with indigenous people. Gradually they formed themselves into loose federations for protection and trade. It was during this period of late Bronze Age and early Iron Age that the first hill forts appeared. Weapons were hoarded as a sign of status and wealth in the community and it was not long before it was realised another means of trading was needed. A form of currency based on the sword was introduced widely in the South about 200BC. Sword shaped currency bars were the forerunner of the gold coin or 'stater' introduced to Britain from France and Belgium (Gaul) around the mid-second century BC.

Within the Andover rural district are a large number of Iron Age sites including three hill forts – Danebury, Bury Hill and Balksbury – some of which existed well into the Roman period. An excavation at Vigo Road by the local archaeological society found a rectangular-shaped, ditched settlement and the nearest Iron Age site to the centre of Andover, close to the church in an area now partly covered by the Silkweavers Road housing estate. It was a large site and would have stretched from New Street across Vigo Road and the recreation ground and bowling green.

Old Down Farm, Andover, was another sub-rectangular shaped enclosure and was excavated by the Test Valley Archaeological Committee, under the direction of Sue Davies and with help from the local society. Old Down Farm turned

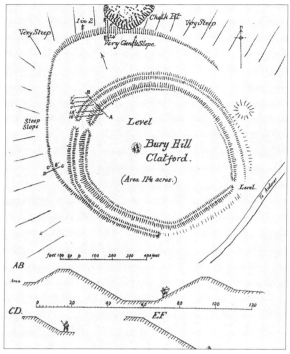

8. Plan of Bury Hill Iron Age hill fort (from 'An Introduction to Field Archaeology in Hampshire' by J P Williams-Freeman, 1915).

out to be a ditched site on high ground, close to a good water supply and the Harrow Way. It revealed settlement from the late Neolithic period to the pagan Saxon period. Evidence shows that most of the settlements in the area were built on high ground near to a good water supply. This may be because the valleys were used for growing crops and grazing cattle with the rivers marking tribal or community boundaries.

It is difficult to say just how far the sites in the area were dependent upon each other or even in contact, but it is quite possible that some specialised in such things as horses or sheep, and exchanges and trading would have occurred. Many hill forts were sparsely occupied and may only have been intended as places to collect and corral animals at various times of the year. Balksbury, just north of the Andover bypass and adjacent to Salisbury Road, is suggested as being a good example of such a site, as are the small banjo-shaped enclosures in the area such as at Blagden Copse, near Hurstbourne Tarrant, excavated by I.M. Stead in 1961.

THE HILL FORTS

Gradually these early hilltop enclosures went out of use and by the sixth century BC a number of smaller, stronger forts were built in central Wessex. In the area around Andover, we know of four – Danebury, Figsbury, Bury Hill and Quarley Hill. The size and strength of the defences all suggest that they were each the centre of a distinct territory and provided protection for the growing community.

Danebury, approximately six miles south-west of Andover, was perhaps the more important in the area, the tribal centre. It was considered important enough for a major excavation to be carried out by Professor Barry Cunliffe over some 18 years, from 1969. The earthworks, with their massive forward looking hornworks, are most impressive at the entrance, being about 17m from the ditch to the top of the rampart. Near the entrance a pile of 11,000 slingshot stones were found. Originally there would have been two entrances but the west gate was blocked in around 400BC as part of a grand strengthening of the defences.

Inside, a community existed of between 300 and 500 people. In the centre were four rectangular structures, probably shrines or holy places. Circular houses clustered around the perimeter of the fort close to the inner rampart from which they may have gained some protection from the weather. The grain stores were massive square buildings, probably made from timber with a wattle infill and long-term grain storage would have been in some of the 5000+ pits found within the defended area. Amongst the buildings various craftsmen, including potters, weavers, leatherworkers, blacksmiths and bronze smiths, worked.

There is a great deal of evidence to show that the Iron Age community which lived at Danebury traded far and wide. Gold, copper and iron came from Wales and the south west; tin came from Cornwall; quern stones for grinding corn came from the Sussex Weald; Kimmeridge Shale which came from Dorset was used for the manufacture of armlets, beads and other decorative items and salt was brought either from the Hampshire and Dorset coasts or from the Droitwich area. A hoard of 21 currency bars was found bundled in a pit near the south ramparts, showing that iron was traded, and a small number of gold staters over

9. *Danebury Iron Age hill fort from the air, excavated by Professor Barry Cunliffe over an 18-year period from 1969.*

the site suggest that these were used for as a currency.

The full story of the development of an Iron Age community based on Danebury is now told in a new Museum of the Iron Age, situated adjacent to Andover Museum in Church Close. It is considered a museum of international importance and the largest of its kind in Europe. Andover Museum houses many other finds from the area including those from the Chilbolton Burial. The ground floor has four galleries, one of which outlines the geology of the area; another has an aquarium stocked with fish typical of the chalk streams around Andover and an extremely realistic natural history display showing the flora and fauna of the chalk landscape. The remaining ground floor galleries house temporary and visiting displays to the Museum. The upper galleries include the archaeology gallery dedicated to Max and Peggy Dacre, the founders of Andover Archaeological Society, whilst the remaining galleries explain the history of Andover in chronological order.

Numerous other late Iron Age settlement sites

exist in the Andover area including Knights Enham Hill, which shows signs of later Roman occupation and possibly Saxon. A fairly large settlement appears to have escaped excavation in the area now covered by Blendon Drive and Chaucer Avenue. Earlier air photographs show tell-tale traces of a large ditched enclosure as well as the lines of boundary ditches of an Iron Age farming system. A small archaeological dig in the garden of one of the archaeological society's members turned up a considerable amount of material that was recovered and recorded, including the footings of a Roman building.

Another site that missed full excavation was known as Spine Road. It occupied an area between the present day Twining's factory and Admiral's Way Estate. The discovery of this site was made in 1964 when road-making machines began cutting a route for a new spine road from the A303 to Walworth Road roundabout. Innumerable pits, a large corn-drier and other features were revealed, and spontaneous outcries against the destruction of the site from the residents of the town led to the Andover Archaeological

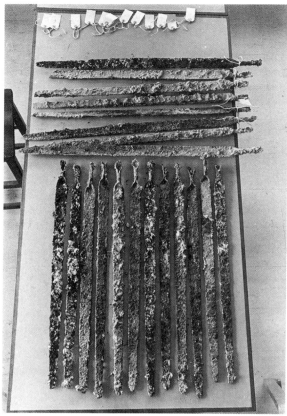

10. Currency bars found in a pit near the south ramparts of Danebury hill fort.

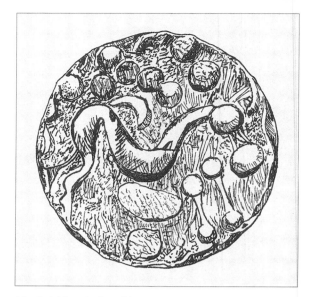

11. British coin found in 1969 at Danebury Hill. (Stater – Gallo-Belgic C type, c.100-70BC)

Society being formed.

As the footings of the present footbridge were being made a boundary ditch was cut through – this can still be seen today in some weather conditions. A quantity of Roman pottery including wine amphorae was discovered amongst even earlier fingertip decorated pottery of the 6th century BC. This site lies within yards of the Icknield Way, a Roman road running from *Venta Belgarum* (Winchester) to *Cunetio*, near Mildenhall in Wiltshire.

At Tinkers Hill, Finkley Down, Iron Age pottery and a brooch have been found on a site known to be have been used well into the Roman period. A small settlement was found at High View Farm, Kimpton, that was also occupied well into the Roman period. An Iron Age currency bar was amongst the finds made on this site dug by the archaeological society.

THE ORIGIN OF THE NAME 'ANDOVER'

The name Andover is Celtic in origin, being made from '*afon*' (river) and '*dwfr*' a generic water word making 'Afondwfr'. 'Afon' was pronounced 'Oun' by some tribes in Britain and this was often corrupted into Oune, Owen and even Onna and Anna. 'Dwfr' has become corrupted into defer, dever and dover. Dever survives to this day in the river of that name running through Micheldever and which joins the River Test at Wherwell. The Anna or Ann, once the name of the river that runs through the town, was known in the sixteenth century as the Westbrook and later still as the Anton, the name it retains to this day. This is an antiquarian fiction, due to the name Antona in a passage of Tacitus, relating to Britain, wrongly suggested as the Test or Itchen.

The Ann was also once the name of the stream running through Abbotts Ann, now known as the Pillhill Brook and which still occurs in the place names of several of the villages nearby. In the early Anglo-Saxon period it was very common to place a preposition before nature-names, generally 'aet', literally meaning at or by, which was an expression for homestead or settlement. 'Aet Andeferan' would therefore signify the settlement at the An Water. Later spellings are 'Andovere' (1086), 'Andever' (12th-18th centuries) 'Andevere' and 'Andovere' (13th century).

Romans, Saxons and Vikings

THE ROMAN INVASION

Roman influence in Britain did not take effect suddenly when Julius Caesar first raided in 55 BC. The Belgic and Germanic tribes had been under Roman influence for a number of years prior to their emigration to Britain and they brought with them Roman ideas and methods. These people traded heavily with Gaul and Romanised Europe. In exchange for the commodities for which Britain was famous – metals (lead, tin, some gold and silver), slaves for the Roman consumer market, hides and hunting dogs – they imported Italian wines for the aristocracy, fine pottery, amber, ivory and raw glass.

During the 1st century BC in the south of England a different type of culture was beginning to develop. Large market centres were emerging and the communities of Hampshire and East Sussex began to form closer political and economic ties with their neighbours across the Channel in Upper Normandy. The lifestyles of those in the south gradually imitated their more advanced allies.

In the Andover area it was Danebury that appears to have taken on the duties of the local market centre. After some local trouble around 100BC when the inner gate was burnt down it appears that the permanent population of the hill fort was greatly reduced. It did remain occupied however but little maintenance was done on the site and the metalled roadway showed deep cart ruts. Considerable quantities of wine amphorae, flagons and some Gallo-Belgic coinage have been found from this period. One of the coins was of King Verica; another was attributed to the Durotriges tribe that occupied Dorset while another was of the type 'Gallo-Belgic C', normally associated with the local Atrebates tribe of which Verica was king.

Verica was the last king of the Atrebates tribe. After some local trouble within his kingdom he fled to Rome to ask for assistance, an act which no doubt hastened the Roman invasion of AD43. There is little to suggest that the people of the area including Danebury offered any resistance to the Romans when the Legio II Augusta, under the command of Vespasian arrived. Central

12. *Town at the Roman crossroads – typical scene at a Roman market. Could this have once been the scene at 'Leucomagus' (East Anton)?*

Wessex seems to have been reasonably peaceful and there is little evidence of the army's passage through the area, save for the occasional pieces of military equipment like the spur that was found at Cleave Hill (2.5 miles east).

A TOWN AT THE ROMAN CROSSROADS

Two Roman roads cross the Andover area at East Anton – the Port Way from Salisbury (*Sorbiodonum*) to Silchester (*Calleva*) and the Icknield Way from Winchester (*Venta*) to Mildenhall (*Cunetio*). There are many signs of Roman activity at or near to these crossroads and for years it was believed that a large settlement existed here. During the late 1960s the crossroads site was designated an area for town expansion, and the Andover Archaeological Society under the direction of Mr W. Startin and Mr R. Davies began a small scale excavation after field walking had produced large quantities of second and third century coins.

Further minor excavations proved the site to be of great archaeological significance and possibly a market area or small town. Unfortunately the order was given for the developer to move in, the site was levelled and the Roman Way housing estate built on it. Roman coins are still found from time to time in the area, which may yet yield up some of its secrets. Archaeologists have recently named the site as *Leucomagus* and suggest it may well have been of great significance, but as the site is now virtually built over we may never know for sure.

For many years various maps marked the position of a Roman Station at nearby Finkley Down, from information supplied by Sir Richard Colt-Hoare. In 1867 a 1st century Roman building at Tinkers Hill, Picket Piece was excavated; coins from the first to the fourth century were present as well as numerous other finds including a jug, a signet ring, a fine bronze fibula and innumerable roof nails. It was considered at that time to be an inn or *diversorium*.

ROMAN VILLAS

Andover is surrounded on all sides by Roman villas or 'farm estates' and indeed two mosaics taken from villas at Thruxton and Abbotts Ann can be seen at the British Museum. In central Andover in 1936, during the building of the Savoy cinema in London Street, the footings of a Roman building were found complete with hypocaust. In 1984, during building work at the junction of Eastern Avenue with Winchester Street, Roman graves were discovered. The Test Valley Archaeological Trust excavated nine graves in the same area, with various burial goods including weapons, coins, a bone comb and pottery, dating the cemetery to between AD270 and AD390. The closeness of these graves to the Roman buildings

13. A Roman hypocaust (underfloor heating) was usually associated with a bath-house. One like this was found during the building of the Savoy Cinema in London Street in 1936.

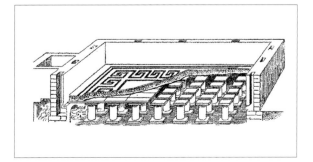

under the Savoy site and to the crossroads at East Anton suggest a busy picture of Roman activity in the Andover area.

Half a mile north-west of Weyhill, at a villa site in Appleshaw parish, a hoard of 4th-century Roman pewter vessels was found, one bearing a Christian monogram, the 'Chi-Rho' symbol.

The Roman influence in Britain declined rapidly toward the end of the 4th century as the legions gradually left. Life in the towns and villas continued much as before but the economy declined sharply as there were no armies to bolster trade. The period that followed is known to historians as the Dark Ages, due to a severe lack of contemporary written evidence, and we have to rely on archaeologists to fill in some details, mostly based on grave goods and weapons.

THE SAXONS

It is believed that a number of Saxon mercenaries were called in after the protection of the Romans declined, and indeed at Knights Enham Hill, the Andover Archaeological Society discovered a group of human cremations, dating to the early 5th century. Among the finds was a bronze belt buckle of a type worn by soldiers. These were found on a site that could be dated from the Iron Age through the Roman period to the Saxons.

In 1973 the Society began excavating sections of ditch and Bronze Age round barrows on the Portway Industrial Estate when a mechanical excavator unearthed part of a human cranium. It turned out to be the first fragment of the remains of more than 150 Saxon people interred in the area now occupied by a large warehouse. The first skeleton proved to be that of a woman of about 550AD. In the 18 months that followed an area of 6000 square metres was excavated. 69 skeletons were found and more than 70 cremation urns carefully lifted, cleaned and prepared for drawing. Finds included brooches, beads, spears, knives, shields and a bucket, all of which found their way to the Institute of Archaeology at Oxford for cleaning and conservation.

During construction of the link road between Andover and Charlton at Redon Way, a chance discovery of a few pieces of pottery led to a rescue dig by Max Dacre and the AAS. After four months it was established that the site was of Saxon origin and amongst the finds were some 1500 potsherds, numerous loom-weights and weaving tools. A great deal of the site remained under the partially completed road, but the remainder of the deposits lay above a boat-shaped quarry in the chalk, with a flint-surfaced ramp leading down to the lower levels.

Nearby, the Iron Age settlement at Old Down Farm, that had lain abandoned since around AD100, was in use again by the Saxons sometime in the sixth century. They built small rectangular huts with rounded corners and sunken floors, known as *grubenhauser*. These were 2 to 3 metres long and 1.5 to 2 metres wide with a central posthole at either end. The posts, it is presumed, supported a ridge piece for the roofs, which were most likely thatched and probably formed a tent-like structure. In all, six huts were found at Old Down Farm and even though a considerable quantity of household refuse was recovered from them it is suggested that they were most probably temporary accommodation for shepherds.

The pottery found in the huts was fragmentary and of poor quality and the amount of metal was small. A simple bone comb was however found in the *grubenhauser*. It has been suggested that this farm may have been an outlying settlement from the larger site at Charlton link road. The site was abandoned after the Saxon period and returned to farming until required for housing as the Artists Way estate.

Weyhill, west of Andover and not far from the Saxon cemetery at Portway Industrial Estate, may have been the site of a pagan temple, for an early form of the name *Weoh ealth* means a shrine or holy place. Many of the settlements in the immediate area surrounding Andover have place names of Saxon origin. The most obvious example is Charlton or 'Ceorls town' – a ceorl or churl was a free peasant ranking above a serf, obliged to do military service and to keep up bridges and defences. Wherwell, where we read later of an abbey being set up, derives its name from *Hwerwyl* – *hwer* meaning cauldron or bubbling and *welle* meaning springs.

THE VIKING RAIDS

Archaeological evidence of Christian Saxons in the Andover area is scant, although later writings allude to them. It is certain that there was a Christian church in Andover prior to the reign of Ethelred II (978-1016). Perhaps they moved downhill to Foxcotte where we are also told that a church existed at the time of the Domesday Survey in 1086.

Viking raids on Britain began at the end of the 8th century in the north of the country and gradually around the coasts. By the 830s they brought small armies and marauded whole regions. Rich

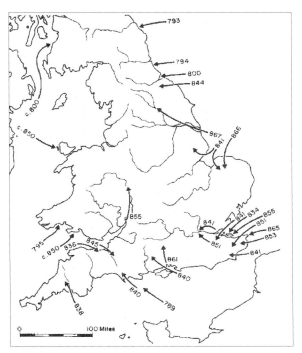

14. *Map showing the Viking attacks around the coast of Britain.*

pickings attracted even more armies until the 850s saw a strong force of 300 ships intent on conquering the whole country. They almost succeeded for it was only King Alfred who held out in the southern kingdom of Wessex. The country was partitioned and the north and east became Danelaw, an area colonised and ruled by Danes and Norwegians.

A few incursions were made into Hampshire as far as Winchester in 860, but they were met with force and routed. Occasional incursions continued for a while until a period of peace, whilst the battles were fought on the continent and at sea. A period of relative calm in southern England followed a number of battles in which the Northmen were forced back into northern England.

'THE 'DANISH DOCK'

Just down-river from Andover at Longstock is an earthwork of a totally different kind to those described previously. It has been suggested by a number of archaeologists including Dr Williams-Freeman that it is an entrenchment put up to conceal and protect a harbour containing ships – a place where they could be laid up and re-

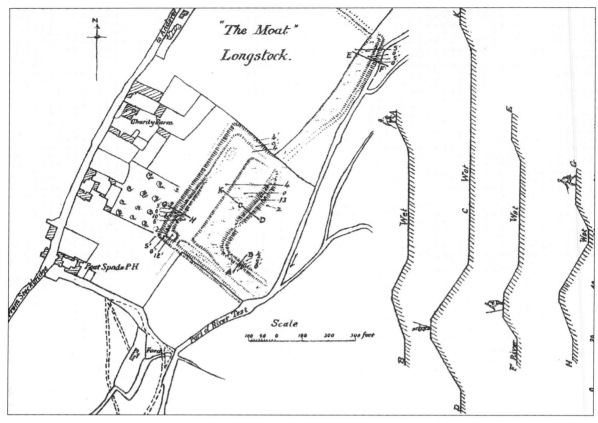

15. *The Danish Dock at Longstock (from 'An Introduction to Field Archaeology in Hampshire' by J P Williams-Freeman, 1915).*

paired. Comprising a well-marked bank and ditch over 3 metres high, the earthworks form three sides of a square of 140-metre sides, the fourth side being formed by the river. Features inside include a concealed entrance to the actual harbour all tending to suggest this is of Danish origin. This then may be the highest point up the River Test which the Viking ships could negotiate. Further research is being done on the site and future archaeologists may be able to give us a better insight of the people who used the earthworks.

THE ROYAL HUNTING LODGE
King Edgar came to the throne in AD958 and spent much of his time in Hampshire and at the capital, Winchester. He was often at the royal hunting seat or 'vill' at Andover, set up by an earlier king referred to in Saxon times as *aet*

Andefera. It is assumed that the lodge was on the high ground overlooking the river somewhere near to the present St Mary's church, but despite numerous archaeological digs little evidence of it has been found. Andover was a convenient centre for the royal hunting forest of Chute and Harewood Forest and under royal protection it was advantageous for traders to spend the night in the area.

Under this royal patronage Andover began to grow in size and importance, its position making it a natural centre for the wool trade. As it grew bodies of craftsmen were able to make a livelihood, making the village virtually self-supporting. The town became a centre for handicraft products and the exchange of agricultural produce. It may also have been under this patronage that the great sheep fair at Weyhill became established.

THE ROYAL COUNCIL OR WITAN

When the King was at Andover hunting lodge, the Royal Council was occasionally summoned to appear before him. The Council or 'Witanegamot' met at Andover in 962 where it was announced that plague had broken out in Edgar's realm and in order to avert the consequences new measures were to be taken to ensure more careful payment of tithes and church taxes.

At a Witan in Andover in 965 it was announced that there was to be an ordinance on the proper treatment of the poor, the sick, and the aged. It placed the duty of the care of these people on their relatives as a Christian duty and required the parishes to see that such care as was necessary was given.

KING EDGAR'S LOVE INTRIGUES

During the Middle Ages the ballad singers amused bystanders at fairs all over the country with stories of King Edgar's love intrigues at Andover. According to Ralph Whitlock, writing in his book *The Warrior Kings of Saxon England*, Edgar arrived in Andover and demanded the beautiful daughter of a local nobleman for a bed-companion. The girl's mother was horrified and substituted a servant girl when it was too dark for the king to notice the difference. The next morning the servant girl got up early to do her usual duties and when asked by the King why she was hurrying she explained that she had her daily chores to do. Edgar then made the servant girl confess the truth after which he considered how to deal with the matter. A short while later he exhorted the servant to be mistress of her former employers, without considering whether they liked it or not.

There is an unsubstantiated legend that Edgar was guilty of killing, with her connivance, the husband of Elfrida, daughter of the Earldorman of Devonshire, so that they could marry. After Edgar's death, driven by remorse, she founded a nunnery at Wherwell where she remained for the rest of her life.

DANEGELD

A second wave of Danish attacks began *c*.980 with raids around the south coast. Organised by leading figures in the Scandinavian world, their intensity increased through the 990s. The first of the great leaders of the Vikings was Olaf Tryggvason, who came over in the raid of 991 that led to the battle of Malden, celebrated by the epic poem of that name. During 993, when he was in the Scilly Isles, Olaf was baptised a Christian, but he continued, along with Sweyn Forkbeard, to plunder the coastal towns.

During the winter of 994, word was passed to Ethelred that Olaf was quartered at Southampton and he went with an army to meet him. Ethelred set up his Court in Andover awaiting developments. On assessing the size of the Viking forces Ethelred decided on negotiation rather than battle and sent Alphege, Bishop of Winchester, to meet Olaf in Southampton and persuade him to meet the King in Andover. Hostilities were halted in return for a 'Danegeld' payment of £16,000. Olaf agreed to return to Norway, never to return as a foe.

When in Andover, Olaf accepted an invitation to be confirmed by Bishop Alphege, suggesting the first reference to a church in the town. Olaf kept his word and returned to Norway the following spring, where shortly afterward he was made the first Christian king of that country. Sweyn however did not feel bound by the agreement made at Andover and continued to plunder Hampshire and the south, being joined by his son Cnut.

Ethelred's problems, far from going away, were increasing and there was genuine fear in the country that with the pressure of Viking incursions the country could lapse into paganism. In 1008 at the King's residence at King's Enham, just north of Andover, was proclaimed:

> I Ethelred the King considered first how I most surely promote Christianity and just Kingship.

This speech was obviously aimed at the Anglo-Saxon bishops who feared the depletion of their power through the alienation of the Church's estates, income and treasures to pay the ever-increasing Danegeld. The last line of the code issued at Enham states:

> We must all love and honour one God and completely cast out every heathen practice. And let us loyally hold to one royal lord, and defend life and land together as well as ever we can, and from our inmost heart beseech Almighty God for help.

Ethelred, leaving the country under his son's protection, went to Normandy to raise new forces to fight the Danes. Cnut succeeded his father in 1013 and only returned to Denmark when Ethelred

16. Canute and Elfgifu, from Stowe manuscripts.

returned the following year. In 1016 Ethelred died, leaving his son Edmund Ironside as his successor. Cnut returned later that year and began to take control of Wessex. A battle is said to have taken place between Edmund and Cnut near Andover at a place called *Sceorstan*. The Rev. Clutterbuck in his book *Notes on the Parishes of Fyfield, Kimpton, etc.* conjectures that the site of this battle would be close to the villages of Weyhill, Amport and Sarson some four or five miles from the town. At the time of the Domesday Survey (1086) the local name for Sarson was 'Soresdene'.

To quote from the writings of a contemporary, Polydore Vergil, an author whom it is known made some mistakes but whose endeavour was to write "a sincere history":

Such haste made Canutus to cope with Edmundus, whom he understood to be returned to Andover, a town within xv miles of Salisberie, whither as soon as hee approached hee planted his tentes on a playne ground within the sight of his enemies and brought his soldiers forth in good arraye. Edmundus refused not the profer as soon as hee espied the standerdes of his adversaries to be hoysed. They continued the fight from iij of the clock until verie night, and neither partie on the better hand; at the length Edricus minding to appal and kill the hearts of the English menn, went up into a certaine watch tower, and then crieing with a high voice that Edmundus was slaine, showed forthe a swoorde droppinge full of blodd, whom, while he thus yelled and shouted, the English archers had near hand slayne. This now being ascended with wonderus indignation, encouraginge his noble warriors, soe furiuslie, assayled them to geve ground, and consequentlie, as altogether enraged, hee put them all to flight, and had committed wonderful slaughter if they hadd not been verie swift, and the night verie dark and farr spente. Canutus being thus foyled travayled all the night toward Winchester, and borrowed himself in a safe place.

Local historians have suggested that Cnut's camp was the Iron Age hill fort of Bury Hill at Upper Clatford. A short while after this battle the two kings agreed to share the kingdom between them, until an act of treachery led to Edmund's murder and Cnut was proclaimed sole king of England. Odd finds over the last thirty years or so in the gardens, and when a footpath was being laid in Mead hedges, suggest a running battle fought in this area of Andover. Unfortunately, these finds did not find their way into the hands of archaeologists and were not officially recorded and evaluated.

Domesday and Beyond

Shortly after the Norman invasion and Battle of Hastings in 1066, Winchester submitted to the rule of William the Conqueror who, from there, began his campaigns to subdue and unite the nation. Soon Andover was established as a Royal Manor with its lands and rights belonging to the king. It was this possession that gave rise to the lion later being incorporated in Andover's coat of arms. The lion is shown standing under the oak tree, symbolising the royal forests of the Saxon kings. As small as it was, Andover was effectively regarded as a town, with all the relevant appurtenances.

The *Anglo-Saxon Chronicle* recorded that at Gloucester in 1085, William I

....had a deep search with his counsellors ....and sent men all over England to each shire ... to find out ... what or how much each landowner held ... in land and livestock, and what it was worth ... The returns were brought to him.

What is now known as the Domesday Survey was completed in 1086. It recorded that:

The King holds Andovere in demesne, King Edward held it. They have not stated the number of hides Land for ..... . In demesne are 2 ploughs. There are 62 villeins, and 36 bordars, and 3 coliberts, and 6 serfs, with 24 ploughs. There are 6 mills worth 72 shillings and 6 pence; and 18 acres of meadow, woodland worth 100 swine from the pannage.

Of the six mills mentioned only four of these can be sited with any certainty. They are Cricklade Mill, Town Mill (which today survives as a public house), Anton Mill and Rooksbury Mill (still surviving).

No reference was made to a church but it has been well proved that one existed in Andover at the time of the Conqueror's arrival. Sometime between 1086 and 1089 the church of Andover and the chapel at Foxcotte were granted to the Abbey of St Florent, at Saumur in Normandy. A copy of the grant survives in France which records the event:

Let it be known to those present and to come that William, king of the English, has given to

17. *The Town Mills, Andover. One of six mills mentioned in the Domesday Survey (photograph taken 1990).*

18. *Andover's Norman parish church, south side. It was originally dedicated to St Peter but after it burnt down during the Civil War in 1141, it was re-dedicated to St Mary.*

God and St Florent the church of Andover, with its tithes and all its appurtenances, as it was at the time of King Edward, and he directs that ythe churches built under the mother church of Andover should be utterly destroyed, or should be held by the monks of St Florent.

Wihenoecus, monk of St Florent, and William the monk, Count Alan and Ivo Tailbois, then witnessed the grant. The Abbey installed a Prior at Andover and two monks to look after the spiritual needs of the community. They occupied buildings erected on the north side of Andover Church, farming the church lands and attending to the interests of the parent abbey in Anjou. The monks, subject to the approval of the Abbot and the Bishop of Winchester, chose the Vicar of Andover.

CIVIL UNREST

The peace and order that accompanied Henry I's reign ended with his death in 1135. He had already indicated that the throne should pass to his daughter, Matilda, and she was accepted at the Christmas Court of 1126/7. However, news of the king's death reached her cousin Stephen while he was in Boulogne and, seizing the opportunity, he set sail for England to claim the crown. Within three months he was anointed king. Matilda's plans were thus thwarted and despite her representations to Rome, Stephen retained the throne.

Civil unrest broke out in all parts of the kingdom and this was accelerated when Matilda crossed the Channel in 1139 with an army. A major battle took place at Lincoln, in which the king was taken prisoner. In her bid to become queen Matilda set out to gain the support of the bishops. Her biggest hurdle was Henry, Bishop of Winchester who was also Stephen's brother. He agreed to meet her at Wherwell in 1141 and terms were established whereby she should enter the city of Winchester, where the crown would

19. St Mary's parish church and churchyard before 1820.

be handed over to her. Despite winning over several other church leaders, her good fortune did not last. Stephen's queen (also called Matilda) chased her out of London and back to Winchester Castle. By this time the Bishop of Winchester had changed sides again and Matilda besieged him at the castle of Wolvesey in Winchester. At the same time, in order to maintain communications with her supporters in Oxford, she garrisoned Andover and the nunnery of Wherwell in order to hold 'the passage of the Test'.

ANDOVER SET ON FIRE

As a consequence, when the forces of Stephen's queen confronted Matilda, they burnt Andover and the nunnery at Wherwell and went on to chase her from Winchester after besieging the city for three weeks. Very little detail survives regarding the burning of Andover other than that the damage was so considerable it affected trade for many years. The church was burnt to the ground and after the war its dedication was changed from St Peter to that of St Mary. Royal help was given to the town to help it rebuild.

THE MERCHANT GUILD

By 1175 merchants in Andover had formed themselves into a guild, and made application to the King to confirm its status on similar terms to those existing in Winchester and Salisbury, upon payment of 10 marks. The Andover Guild of Merchants and its early morning meetings, known as 'morrow speech', became the town's earliest form of self-government.

King John granted what is perhaps the most important of the medieval charters to the burgesses of Andover on 18 April 1201 upon payment of 20 marks and a palfrey (a palfrey was a saddle horse for riding). The use of the term burgesses suggests that by then Andover had developed into a Borough and was considered as such by the Crown. The charter granted to the burgesses the town's 'fee farm' (the right to collect borough rents in exchange for a single payment to the Crown), together with the right to collect 'quit rents' (a payment which excused the tenant from the services to a feudal lord – in this case, the burgesses), in return for another annual payment to the Crown.

John confirmed this charter on 1 May 1205 and

again later in the month when he added the right for the burgesses to hold a fair each year, on the festival of St Leonard (4-6 November). It is not known when Andover market began though it and the fair both came under the auspices of the Guild of Merchants. The market, which expanded a great deal in the Middle Ages, traded in cattle, sheep, corn and cheese. Another important fair was held at Weyhill at Michaelmas, specialising in sheep, held on the downs near the church. Also dealing in cattle and leather, it was not long before it rivalled the south of England's other great fair at St Giles's Hill, Winchester.

In another charter of 31 October 1213, King John granted the Guild merchants the right to hold an In Hundred and Out Hundred (or 'Foreign') court, giving them legal jurisdiction over an area covering the fifteen villages surrounding the town. The charter confirmed the right of the 'Men of Andover' to collect the rents due to the Crown and pay it in one sum. Known as the fee farm, it went directly into the king's treasury. This was again confirmed in 1256 in another charter, adding that all letters should be addressed to the Merchant Guild, thus bypassing the function of the Sheriff of Hampshire. The In and Out Hundred courts heard the presentments of local landowners, dealing with land and property disputes and petty crimes. It was also the basis of the town returning members of Parliament.

The right of the Guild to govern Andover was based purely upon these charters and by custom. It was confident enough by the time of a 'Morrow speech' in 1415, to announce:

> It was ordained at the said morrow speech with the consent of the same vill that the twenty-four shall be elected there and shall have the government of the said vill under the supervision of the stewards and Bailiffs for the time being...

The Guild was not averse to handing out punishment should any member break its rules and in 1327 it threw out of the guild Robert le Kyllere for telling lies to the members, suggesting that 55 men would be ready to rob and destroy them. It was decided by the whole meeting that no one would ever acknowledge his existence again, or supply him with anything, under penalty of loss of guild membership. When it was later found his mother had gone to his aid, it was announced she would be fined 20 shillings if she offended again.

Records of the Guild show that they looked after themselves very well, as this excerpt from their 'morrow speech' in 1338 records:

> Stewards' allowances. Each steward shall have each day four gallons of ale, though the light ale may be five gallons – granted. Likewise, each cupbearer shall receive from the testers each day six loaves and on each day six loaves and on each day ivd. each of them. Clerks' allowances. Each shall have each day two gallons of ale and from the tasters each six loaves each day, and on each day iii d, each. Tasters' allowances. All of them one gallon of ale."

The Guild continued to administer Andover until the town was granted a charter by Elizabeth I in 1599.

THE FORESTS OF THE SAXON KINGS

The forests of the Saxon kings that once surrounded Andover were gradually reduced in size as the land was used for agriculture and sheep pasturage. Andover and Finkley Forest were part of the much larger Chute Forest, which extended into Wiltshire. References of royal gifts from this forest are numerous from the time of Henry III.

> 1245 – To the Bailiffe of Andevre – contrabreve to carry the timber of one-hundred oaks which the King has felled in the Forest of Finkele to Freimantel without delay for delivery to the keeper of the King's works there.

Freemantle Park in Kingsclere parish was once another of the royal hunting lodges of the Norman kings during the 12th and 13th centuries, which became classed as a manor at the time of Edward I.

As rebuilding work continued on Winchester Castle after its burning in 1141, there were many requests for timber and in the records of Chute Forest at Doles Wood and Finkley for the years between 1232 and 1235 are many references for timber to mend "the hall", for "making a certain new Kitchen", a "butlery and dispensary", a "turret and chamber over". Timber was also needed for the drawbridge and the "King's saucery" (a sauce and spice store).

In 1229 the monks of the priory of St Florent at Andover made a request to Henry III for timber to repair the building on account of a recent fire there. In 1333 Edward III imposed one of his court officials, John Baddeby, on the Prior, who was ordered to provide him with hospitality for as long as he lived. The same king later ordered John

Wyght of Kingston, his sergeant, to be allowed to spend the rest of his days there in such comfort as there might be.

THE HARROW OR PILGRIMS' WAY
The Harrow Way passed Andover at the foot of New Street and at its junction a travellers' hospice was situated, dedicated to St John the Baptist. This was probably established during the reign of William I. It received a royal charter in 1247 and in the same year the Andover Merchants' Guild granted it 50 shillings for the maintenance of a chaplain. There has been much conjecture as to where St John's House stood but it is almost certain to have been on the site of the Blacksmith's Arms public house.

It has been suggested that the Harrow Way or Pilgrims' Way was diverted through Andover early in the 13th century and the hospice placed where it was in order to cater for the pilgrims on their journey to the shrine of St Thomas at Canterbury. During the 16th century the section of the Harrow Way we know today as Watery Lane, between the Approach garage and the Churchill Way Trading Estate, was known as St John's Lane.

In 1250 the brethren and sisters were licensed to enclose a piece of land belonging to the King, opposite the hospital, to build a chapel for the celebration of divine service. Many references are made in the Guild records to the Hospice of St John from 1262 when Roger Chit (the small) was ordered to pay 13 shillings to the chaplain of the hospital. There appears to have been a vineyard at the house for in 1284 "By the decision of the Gildsmen, Master Adam Richmond has the vineyard at the House of St John for his whole life for 12 pence to be paid to the brothers and sisters of the said house". The Guild records also show that in 1309 John the Shoemaker, who was also a priest at the Hospice, was ordered to collect two pounds of wax from Geoffrey the Thresher and his wife for the purpose of keeping a light on the altar of St John the Baptist.

ANDOVER WOOL
During the early years of the 12th century Andover was becoming well known as a centre for the clothing industry along with other towns such as Bristol, Winchester, Marlborough, Bedwyn, Cricklade and Reading. The area was well suited to the rearing of sheep. Many of the valleys flooded during the winter months, producing lush grass. By the end of the fifteenth century the largest

20. Hand-loom weaving. Under the guild system in Andover, the employer supplied the raw material to family units to process.

owner of sheep and trader in wool was the Bishop of Winchester.

In 1272 nine Andover merchants were given the right to export wool. These included Alexander le Riche, who was allowed to export 44 sacks; two years earlier le Riche (Bailiff of Andover in 1263) travelled with other merchants to Flanders to make enquiries about goods supplied by them and to claim monies owed.

Weaving and cloth production became an important element of the town's commerce. The medieval records of the Hampshire Aulnager – the officer responsible for ensuring that any cloth sold was woven to the right measurements and quality – have many references to Andover and Whitchurch weavers producing, in particular, kerseys, a coarse narrow cloth woven from long wool. J.H. Bettey's book *Wessex from 100AD* notes that in return for the export of cloths and dyestuffs to Genoa, Florence and Venice, Andover was receiving large quantities of wine.

The system of cloth production practised by Andover merchants was to supply raw material to journeymen or apprentices who would then arrange for processing by finishers, fullers and dyers. The finished cloth was then passed back to the merchants for sale.

An example of Andover's prominence in the wool exporting market comes from a Close Roll, dated 1297:

> John de Penynton merchant of Andovere lately delivered eight sacks of wool to the keeper of the King's new custom at Southampton by way of pledge for 47li.3sh.2d. to be paid to them at Whitsummer next for the custom due from him for the sack taken by him from the port of Southampton to Flanders. Simon de Greenhull whom the King lately selected to arrest wool and hides in that county took the 8 sacks for the King's use but now they are restored to the Merchant.

THE KNIGHTS OF ST JOHN

The small community of Knights Enham, just two miles north of the town, was so named as the manor was owned for a period during the thirteenth century by the religious order known as the Knights Hospitaller or Brethren of St John of Jerusalem. Their members wore a black cloak, with a white cross upon the left breast. The surplus revenue from their estates was sent to Palestine to help pay for the relief of the battleworn and weary Crusaders and the protection of pilgrims to the Holy Land.

In 1280, the tenant of the Knights Hospitaller land at Enham, Hugh de Evinley, was summoned to show cause why he had failed to attend a Hundred court at Andover. He pleaded that by a charter granted by Henry III to the Prior and Brethren of the Order of St John of Jerusalem, the Prior and his men were freed from all fines and taxes and service at the Hundred court and he argued that as the land he held was theirs he need not attend.

MPs FOR ANDOVER

Andover sent two Members of Parliament to Westminster from 1295 to 1307, but due probably to financial constraints, the writs of 1309 and 1311 were ignored. From then Andover remained unrepresented in Parliament until 1586 when the town was again included in the list of Hampshire representatives.

ST FLORENT PRIORY

During the long-war against the French an attempt was made by the Bishop of Winchester in 1341 to sequestrate the funds of St Florent priory in Andover to his own treasury. He was sharply rebuked by the King and in 1360, after the war, the King regranted the priory to the Abbey of St Florent in France. However, during the reign of Henry V, Parliament agreed to the dissolution of alien priories and St Florent was granted to Winchester College instead.

THE COMMON ACRE

The Common Acre, now incorporated into the recreation ground in Vigo Road was, in theory, a place for common recreation. It was leased out by the town for pasture, but, as the earliest known lease of 1470 notes, the tenants were "to allow everyone of good governance to play at spears and arrows and other games". The 'Benefactions Tablet' in St Mary's church (*see ill.21 and p.48*) indicates that the Acre was given to the town in 1570 by spinster Katherine Hanson, whereas we know that it was leased by the town from at least 1470 until the mid-19th century.

Archery butts were located on the Acre. When the lease went to Thomas Aldred in 1513 it was stipulated that he was to set up butts there and in 1540, when the lease was changed again, it was noted that the butts were "anciently accustomed". Their frequent use was confirmed in 1542 when Henry VIII made an order that able-bodied men

ANDEVER
THE NAMES OF THE BENEFACTO[r]
OF THIS TOWNE, W[th] THEIR GUIFTS, WHEN &FOR
WHAT VSES GIVEN
BY EDWARD WARHAM GENT BAYLIFFE
ANNO DNI 1692.

An: 1569 IOHN HANSON of this Towne gent gaue 200[li] out of y profit of which mony is to be paid yearly for the Founding & towards y mayntenance of the Freeschoole in this towne to the fchoolmafter thereof 16[li]

An 1570 KATHERIN HANSON spinster gaue y ground called Comon Acre for the Recreation of the Inhabitants of this towne

1598 RICHARD VENABLES Cittizen & marchant Taylor of London gaue 100[li] for to provide 13 two penny loaves of Bread for 13 poore people of this towne in y Church of Andover every sunday in the year for ever.

1600 ANDEVER CORPORATION added 2 two peny loaves to be forever weekly delivered with the 13 loaves giuen by M[r] VENABLES

1611 RICHARD KEYMYS of this towne gent. gaue 400[li] to purchafe twelve pounds per Ann to be difpofed of in maner following vi: 5[li] yearly to provide twelve two peny loaves of Bread weekly 50 weeks in the yeare for y poore on sunday morning in the Church. Other 5[li] yearly to be diftributed to the poore in mony on Good fryday, Other 5[li] yearly to be paid to the schoolmafter of y Freeschoole in Andover. Other 5[li] to be yeerely given to a Lecturer befides y minifter & when there is noe Lecturer that Five pounds to be yearly given to the poore in mony on Afh wednefday. HEE LIKEWISE gaue 40[li] to buy Ornam[t] for Andever Church, & 10[li] to buy a fair Callice of Silver guilt for the Comunion. HEE LIKEWISE gaue One Hvndred pounds to pave & repair the High street & other streets in Andover.

1622 THOMAS WESTCOMBE Cittizen & Leather fellar of London gaue a little peice of ground whereon a Barne formerly stood to provid eighteen peny Loaves of Bread every Quarter day or sunday next following to be given to 18 poor people quarterly by sexton of Andover to have y advantage of the faid Bread

1624 PETER BLAKE of y Inner Temple London Efq gaue a rent charge of six pounds per Ann iffuing out of his Tenem[t] in Andever to be payd to y poore of Andover & two other parifhes of which Andover is to have the greateft part.

1628 RICHARD BLAKE of this Towne gent. gaue 30[li] The Interest of it to be paid for ever to the poore on good fryday. HEE LIKEWISE gaue to this Towne y land whereon the Freefchoole is built.

1631 IOANE BLAKE WIDDOW & Relict of the fayd M[r] RICHARD Blake gaue 30[li] to be difpofed of like maner as her late hufbands Thirty pounds.

1610 THOMAS CORNELIUS of London Marchant By will gaue to y poore of this Towne y Interest of it to be given yearly in mony on Goodfryday.

1633 M[rs] MARY VENABLES of Bafingftoke spinster by will gave to y poore of this town 5[li]

1633 MICHAELL PEASLEY of this towne Appothecary by will after his debts Legacyes & Funeralls difcharged gaue the refidue of his goods & Chattells to y poore of this Towne, w[ch] Amounted to & was received 35[li] & difpofed of by y y Corpor[on]

1634 GEORGE PEMBERTON one of the Aldermen of y City of winchefter gaue to this towne 100[li] to pay to the poore fix pounds Thirteen fhillings & foure pence yearely for ever on S[t] THOMAS day. & S[t] George y martyr by equall portions

1625 WALTER WAITE of this Towne gent. gave 20[li] per Ann to the poore of this towne to be paid out of Brownes tenement in Andover.

1650 RICHARD IAY of Reading gent. gave to the poore of this towne 100[li] the product to be yearly diftributed amongst the poore.

1658 NICHOLAS FISHBORNE als BEALE of this towne gave to the poore 10[li]

1642 HENRY SMYTH of London Efq gave to the poore of this towne 10[li] per Ann for ever to be yearely received out of lands in Stoughton in Com Leicefter by the Church wardens & overseers of Andover.

1679 THE HON[ble] FRANCIS POWLETT Efq gave to y poor of this place 100[li]

1686 IOHN POLLEN Efq erected Founded & Endowed an HOSPITALL in this Towne for fix poore aged men.

1600 M[rs] CHRISTIAN HINXMAN Widdow gaue by deed to y poor of

21. The Benefactions Tablet in St Mary's church.

should practise the skill after Divine Service each Sunday. In 1560 a new lessee, William Good, was required to "kepe make and maynteyne one pair of butts there mete for men to shoote at" and "to suffer all manner of persons to come and goe in to and from the said premises to shote and have theire pastyme there as it hath been accustomed".

Henry VIII's pre-occupation with keeping men skilled at archery was necessary at a time when the country needed archers in its armies. During the French wars musters were made across Hampshire to provide him with men. In March 1523 an army was raised to ravage Picardy and a muster ensured that the In-Hundred of Andover provided 31 archers and 79 billmen, whilst the Out Hundred provided 72 archers and 147 billmen.

When musters occurred during the years 1572-4 it was reported to the Queen that Andover had 70 able men and a further 148 in the Out-Hundred.

THE GREAT FIRE OF ANDOVER

Towards the end of the medieval period, in 1435, virtually all the centre of Andover was destroyed by fire. According to contemporary accounts it began in a butcher's shop in White Bear Yard and engulfed the greater part of the town so that little more than the church and the priory, built of stone, survived. One of the buildings destroyed was the College Inn, on Winchester College land, which was succeeded in 1445 by the Angel. Detailed accounts of the carpenter's work in this new inn still survive at Winchester College – he also worked on Eton College.

The old Angel was threatened with wanton destruction in the 1960s when a new Andover Town Centre was proposed. This involved demolition of the inn, but after a 'Save the Angel' campaign plans were amended and the inn was left outside the redevelopment scheme. The reprieve gave local architectural student Richard Warmington the opportunity to produce drawings showing a complete reconstruction of the Angel, as it would have looked in 1445. He demonstrated that it was twice its present size, built around a square courtyard with galleries at first-floor level. Now, only the north and west wings survive, but it would have extended down the High Street as far as the entrance to the Chantry Shopping Centre.

In 1621 the landlord of the Angel was Richard Pope, Bailiff of Andover and grandfather of the poet Alexander Pope. In 1642 Mrs Marie Pope

22. The Angel Inn in the High Street in 1960 – saved from the bulldozer by a public campaign.

*23. The north wing of the Angel Inn c.1460, soon after
the Great Fire of Andover. Drawn by Richard
Warmington 1968.*

was one of 28 licensees fined 20d for 'not selling the best beere for one penneye'. The Angel at this time was the premier hostelry of the town.

Nine years after the fire the west side of the Upper High Street was still referred to as "void ground". Until the fire the greater part of Andover was clustered on the hilltop near the church, and the principal thoroughfare, which formed part of the London to Salisbury Road, was routed down Vigo Road and Newbury Street and turned in front of the main gateway to the Angel Inn down the High Street. Chantry Street, Marlborough Street, New Street and the Upper High Street were all well developed. The lower High Street was developed after the Fire and a new guildhall built on the site of the present building, probably about 1470. The town accounts of 1513-18 detail repairs made to this building and suggest it was on two levels – upper floor with meeting room, and lower with shops. It was probably after the Fire that the market, held in several streets, was relocated down the High Street to its present position.

Tudor Times

RELIGIOUS FERVOUR AND THE 'BLESSED' JOHN BODY

Elizabeth I's task on coming to the throne in 1558 was to resolve the religious question hanging over the country. The reformation of the Church brought about by Henry VIII had begun to be reversed by her Catholic sister, Mary, but Elizabeth decided to follow in her father's footsteps instead. After a rocky passage through both Houses of Parliament, the Uniformity Bill and the Supremacy Bill were passed and the Queen was made Supreme Head of the Church of England.

Commissioners were sent to every corner of the country and the clergy were requested to take an Oath of Supremacy – those who refused to sign were deprived of their benefices. In the years that followed many Catholics were imprisoned or executed for their protests.

One such execution took place in Andover in 1583 when John Body was hanged, drawn and quartered for denying the Royal Supremacy. Body was born at Wells in Somerset, where his father, a wealthy merchant, was at one time mayor. In 1562 at the age of 13 he was admitted a scholar of Winchester, passing on to New College, Oxford where he became a Fellow in 1568 and Master of Arts in 1576. During Bishop Horne's Visitation to the College shortly after, he and six others were deprived of their Fellowship. The following year he went to the University of Douai, in the Netherlands, to study civil law.

By 1578 he was back in England and became a teacher at a school said to be between Winchester and Andover. Among his pupils was Benjamin Norton, who wrote a book called the *Memorial on the Acts of the Martyrs* when he was later made Vicar for Hampshire, Surrey, Sussex and Berkshire. Norton wrote about John Body:

> Of Mr J. Boddie I can saye that he was my scolemaster a yeere or to beefore his Apprehension at Mr. Archdeacon Shelleye his father's house, where he was taken and Committed by Sr. Richard Norton & C....

Body was arrested at Mapledurham, near Petersfield in 1580 and sent to Winchester Prison where he joined several fellow Catholics, including John Slade who was imprisoned there two years later.

At the Spring Assizes of 1583, Body and Slade were tried for denying the Royal Supremacy and condemned to death as traitors. There must have been a flaw in the proceedings as we next hear of them coming before the Autumn Assizes held in Andover; again both were condemned and transferred back to Winchester. The government decided that the executions should be in two localities: Slade in Winchester and Body in Andover. The execution of Body took place on Saturday, 2 November 1583, though the exact site has not been recorded.

Cardinal Allen wrote a history of Body's execution and in it he states that the magistrate, Sir William Kingsmill, called upon him at the gallows to confess the crime for which he was condemned, in order that the people might know the reasons for which he died. Mr Body then indicated his obedience and fidelity to the Queen in all civil matters but then spoke to the crowd stating:

> Be it known all of you here present, that I suffer death this day because I deny the Queen to be the supreme head of the Church of God in England. I never committed any other treason, unless they will have the hearing of mass or saying 'Hail Mary's' to be treason.

REFORM OF THE GUILD

As seen in the previous chapter, the Guild of Merchants administered Andover, more by prescriptive right than anything else. By the end of Elizabeth's reign, things were to change considerably.

The Guild merchants formed a Common Council comprising a bailiff and 24 'forwardmen' which governed the town. But as trade and the town's traders and merchants grew in number in Tudor times the functions of government began to overwhelm this system. On the advice of Robert Dudley, Earl of Leicester, who was High Steward of Andover, the Guild was divided into three companies: leathersellers, haberdashers and drapers. All other trades were listed under one of these headings – for example, innkeepers were placed with the haberdashers, and apothecaries with the leathersellers. Each company was governed by a master and two wardens and two other members.

Essentially the companies were closed shops, allowing no-one to trade in the town, except at the time of the annual fair, without their permission and unless they had lived in the town for a year, and were householders and married.

24. *Another of the survivors of the 1960s' destruction of the Town Centre – 80a High Street Andover, a 15th century shop still in use as a hairdresser's.*

25. A woodwork class in Andover Grammar School c.1928, a school descended from John Hanson's bequest of 1571.

One member of the Andover Guild, John Hanson, founded a free school in the town. Hanson, a retired and wealthy London merchant, left in his will of 1571 the sum of £200 "for & towardes the maintenance of a Freeschole within the Boroughe and Towne" stipulating that the schoolmaster should be a graduate of either Oxford or Cambridge and be paid at least 16 shillings per annum.

THE TOWN HOUSE

The Autumn Assize of 1583 which condemned John Body to a painful death would have met in the new town or court house. This building replaced the previous guildhall on the same site, and as with the earlier building, it was divided into an upper meeting house and a ground floor for shops.

THE GREAT CHARTER

Elizabeth I granted the town a new charter in 1599 following a petition from Robert, Earl of Essex. This important landmark in the history of Andover confirmed all previous charters but allowed developments which would make for better government. It declared that:

...our Borough or Town of Andevor aforesaid shall hereafter remain a Free Borough of itself. And that the Burgesses and Inhabitants of the said Borough and Town aforesaid may and shall from henceforth be One Body Corporate and Politic in Deed fact and name by the name of the Bailiff Approved Men and Burgesses of the Borough of Andevor.

The Bailiff and Burgesses were then granted the right to have a Common Seal by which they could execute leases and grants and for any other lawful business. Andover Corporation, as it was called, was to comprise one Bailiff, one Escheator, one Clerk of the Market, two Constables, ten Approved Men and twelve Capital Burgesses. The Bailiff was the chief officer of the Borough and through his position was granted the title of ex-officio Lord of the Manor of Andover. Each year he was elected from one of the ten Approved Men of the town and was required to take his Corporeal Oath immediately after election before his predecessor. William Blake, a farmer from East Anton, was appointed as Andover's first Bailiff. More often than not the Bailiff also took the positions of Coroner and Escheator.

As Coroner, the Bailiff was an officer of the Crown and had a number of duties, which included the holding of inquests, determining what was treasure trove etc. An Escheator collected revenues from estates where the tenant had died without heir or where the heir was below age, or where the tenant had committed an offence which had led to the forfeiture of the estate.

John Moore was appointed Steward, a position roughly equivalent to a Borough Secretary with the present Test Valley Borough Council. There was also a deputy or Town Clerk.

The new Corporation was granted the right to hold an assembly and provide or appoint a building as a Town or Guild Hall. At the same time they were empowered to make Laws and Ordinances to the benefit of the townspeople and also to inflict penalties for infringements.

The Great Charter also made recommendations in the case of a Bailiff, Approved Man or any Burgess refusing to accept their nominated position or to take the Oath. Imprisonment was to be the normal punishment for this until such time as the 'offender' was prepared to take up his office and take the Corporeal Oath.

There were several instances when the Corporation invoked just such a punishment for this offence, as the following example shows:

> ....At this day Thos. Staniford and Wm. Holmes now imprisoned and fined £10 apiece for that they being elected to be two of the Approved Men refused to take their oath, paid the fine aforesaid. 10th August, 1608.

Two Justices of the Peace were elected each year from the Approved Men and Burgesses, but somehow the duties nearly always fell upon the Bailiff and the Steward. This gave a great deal of legal power to the town and through the Bailiff a Court was held to try offenders for such crimes as theft, riotous behaviour, extortion etc., but cases of murder or touching the loss of life could not be heard by him, but by the county sheriff.

Andover was granted the right of a weekly market, which it had already exercised from early times. Four fairs were granted to the town: Weyhill at Michaelmas, St Leonard's Fair, a Lent Fair and another on the Feast of St Philip and James. The most important of these was Weyhill, without doubt the largest, and which brought the town the most profit through hiring of standings, the sale of animal fodder and the use of weights and measures.

The charter also granted freedom from tolls of passage through the county and from attendance at courts of the sheriff and many other freedoms. The Bailiff as Clerk of the Market was made responsible for the Assay of Bread, Wine and Ale which regulated the weights, measures and standards to which these commodities were subject. Bakers who sold underweight bread were liable to be drawn through the town on hurdles.

The Great Charter was a triumph for the Men of Andover for they had managed to have it tailored to their own requirements. Furthermore they had somehow managed to have Weyhill Fair included as being in the ownership of the town, enraging the original owners of the fairground site who in fact had only leased land to the town on which the Bailiff placed his tent.

THE PROCESS OF LAW

Since the days of King Alfred the counties had been divided into hundreds and parishes or tythings. The derivation of the term 'hundred' remains uncertain: it is thought originally to have contained a hundred families, or ten tythings or even to contain one hundred taxable hides of land. The King's Shire Reeve or Sheriff was anciently the legal authority in the county and it was his duty to make a circuit of all the hundreds redressing grievances and preserving the common peace. Over the years however his duties were passed down to the justices of the peace in each town, holding court in their own sessions, but the old hundred courts continued to exist, presided over by a legal official or steward.

In Andover's case a sub-steward or Town Clerk was appointed by the Corporation to whose authority the two hundreds of Andover had been granted by charter. At the hundred courts it was usual to conduct a View of Frankpledge, which was in essence an enquiry into lawlessness and neglect within the area of the hundred. It was based on the theory and practice that each member of a community (tything), was responsible for his/her own actions and for those of the others in the group. It was a corporate responsibility to correct any abuse by other members.

These reviews were held twice a year, usually within one month after Easter and again within one month after Michaelmas at a convenient place within the hundred. The Andover district was divided into the In-hundred and the Out-hundred. The In-hundred comprised the town itself and its outskirts on the north and east side and its meetings were held at the Guildhall. The Out-hundred, consisting of the parishes to the south and west from Upper Clatford to South Tidworth, held its meetings at the Guildhall in the autumn, and at Weyhill in the spring. In theory all persons over the age of 12 and under 70 were required at the court and it was the duty of the tythingman (court representative) to ensure attendance was made and to help form a jury, normally consisting of 20 men, though it was often less.

The courts could fine but not imprison offenders, and it was often the case that they would issue a warning first to correct the offence, under penalty of a fine or levy, should no action be taken. If a person came before the courts on several occasions for the same offence or non payment of a fine, it was the duty of the court to issue a distress proceeding, but often the courts were reluctant to do so. The proceedings were beautifully recorded in black ink on parchment. The Andover archives, now held in the Hampshire Record Office, include a large number of parchment rolls relating to the 16th, 17th and early 18th centuries.

In 1600, cases that came before these courts included battery and assault inflicted with a stick (fine 9d); failure to trim the hedges alongside the King's highway; encroachment of the highway by throwing on it refuse (dung, dead carcasses, brushwood etc); failure to maintain bridges and other public property (stocks, butts and boundaries) and also the breaking of the Sabbath. In truth there was very little which did not come before the hundred courts, but the more serious crimes were held over to the Quarter Sessions.

HIGH STEWARD NOMINATES MP FOR ANDOVER

In July 1584, the Earl of Leicester, who had accepted the position of High Steward of Andover, wrote to the Bailiff asking to be allowed to nominate one of the burgesses to the parliament that the Queen was about to summon. He also pointed out that if he was allowed to nominate a second burgess he would absolve the town of any costs and maintenance and pay them himself.

Andover had not returned a member to Parliament since 1307, which Leicester most probably would have been aware of. He however, made every effort to remedy the situation, his letter reads:

> After my hartie commendacons – Whereas it hath pleased her Maiestie to appoint a parliament to be presently called being steward of youre Towne I make bould hartelie to praye you that you will give me the nomination of one of youre Burgesses for the same. And if myndinge to avoide the charges of allowance for the other Burgesse you meane to name anie that is not of yo'r towne yf you will bestowe the nomination of the other Burgesse also upon me I will thank you for it and will appoint a sufficient man and see you discharged of all the charges on their behaulf. I thus bid you right heartilie farewell from the courte the XIIth of October 1584. If you will send me your election with a blank I will putt in the names.
>
> Y'or loving Frende
> R. Leycester"

As can be seen from the letter, this was the way in which the noblemen of the country kept a grip over the parliaments of their time. Robert Leicester, in addition to Andover, was Steward of Great Yarmouth, Kings Lynn, Bristol and Reading. Looking for support for his policy of military intervention in Holland he called upon Andover to send two MPs but they were obliged to reply that the town sent none. At the next Parliament in 1586, Andover was added to the list of Boroughs sending members.

26. Robert Dudley, Earl of Leicester.

Plague, Scandal and Civil War

THE PLAGUE

Bubonic plague, which entered England in 1348, increased in intensity over the following three hundred years and badly affected Andover during the early years of the seventeenth century. In 1603 the town, along with other places in the county, fell victim and received relief for its parishes from the adjoining hundreds. A short while later, Sir George Kingsmill, one of the Justices for the Common Pleas, wrote to the County Justices appealing for special and exceptional help for Andover. The justices ruled however that in their opinion the town had received considerable aid already and that it had its own justices who should be able to deal with a crisis.

In 1605, John Robinson, keeper of the Three Choughs Inn, in Wood Lane (Bridge Street), attempted to conceal the fact that he had plague under the pretence it was a sore boil, and he allowed 25 members of various families to enter his house. When the authorities discovered this they rounded up 94 infected people. Nine pesthouses were set up in the fields to house them and isolate the infection but by the time the Corporation reported the matter to Sir Henry Whithed, Justice for the Andover Division, 18 persons had died and were buried and 46 were still detained. The town further requested that Sir Henry should believe this report and also urge the neighbouring hundreds of Wallop, Longstock, Leckford and Fullerton to hasten their contribu-

27. The bubonic plague. Illustration from Daniel Defoe's 'A Journal of the Plague Year'(1722).

tions as they were a fortnight in arrears.

The plague was so bad that in 1612 the weekly market was moved, for the next two years, to Weyhill in an effort to lessen the need for villagers to go into the town. In the notebooks of the Rector of Weyhill, Dr Randall Sanderson is recorded:

> In ye spring after 9. Elizabeth dyed. i.e., primo Jacobi, when there begun a sore plague in Andover which lasted 2 years and ye streets were green with grass all over; ye market was kept at Weyhill all ye time."

There are several instances of rents for shops going unpaid at this time due to the plague and a great many names in the parish registers of burials on the other side of the churchyard wall or 'burials in the fields'.

> "Widow Webb the mother to Daniel Girdler's wife supposed to die of the plauge was buried privately in Girdler's garden, October 7th 1625."

> "Widow Edmonds dyed of the plauge and was buried in the fields, Oct. 12th."

> "Daniel Girdler dyed of the plauge and was buried in the drove, Oct. 28th."

TRAVEL INNOVATIONS

In 1601 the Privy Council considered Andover to be of sufficient importance to recommend that horses should be provided there for the postal system or else the town be given financial assistance to provide them:

> A letter to Sir Thomas West and Mr Hampden Paulett and the Justices of the Peace in the devision neere the towne of Andevor requiring them to take order that within the neerest devision to the towne of Andevor there maie some good helpe be afforded to the saide town (in respect of their great charge by the often sending by poste) either by furnishing of horses for her Majesty's service or else (which is supposed the best and easiest waye) in yielding contibucion therunto.

The provision of post horses was intended to speed the transit of mail, but as far as travelling speed was concerned it was the exploit of an Andover man, Bernard Calvert, which set the whole country talking in 1619. He set out from St George's Church, Southwark at 3 o'clock one morning, travelled on horseback to Dover, crossed to Calais by boat and then re-crossed the Channel, re-mounted his horse, and arrived back at Southwark at 8pm the same day. It was the first time a journey from London to France and back in the same day had been recorded. Calvert was landlord of the White Horse Inn, which stood on the site of Priory Lodge in Newbury Street.

MURDER OF A BAILIFF

In a State Paper of 26 August 1627 reference is made to three men condemned for killing a 'Bayliffe' at Andover. The three men, Reeve, Wilson and Holland were sentenced to execution but on the day Reeve confessed to the murder and the other two men were reprieved, though sentenced to serve in the army in Ireland for their part in the crime.

The term 'Bayliffe' was used either to denote the Chief Magistrate and head of the Corporation or else occasionally the Steward. Exactly who was murdered is unknown, though it is recorded that William Jarvis was elected Bailiff the previous September and was there the following year when William Blake was elected in his place.

SHIP MONEY

Ship Money, an Elizabethan tax, was re-introduced initially in the seaports during the reign of Charles I. On the pretext that the tax would be used to protect shipping against piracy it was extended in 1635 to all of England. It was a tax the King received directly without the approval of Parliament and which he used to pay for his army and his disagreements with the Scots. As time went by, the tax became more difficult to collect, especially after a test case brought before the Exchequer Court by John Hampden in 1637.

Sir John Oglander of Nunwell in the Isle of Wight who was Sheriff of Hampshire and collector of ship money, reported in 1637 great difficulties in collecting the tax and that the boroughs, especially Winchester, Andover and Southampton, were very reluctant to pay, and that many in the county districts pleaded poverty. The Hampshire towns were assessed as follows: Southampton £195, Winchester £190, Portsmouth £60, Basingstoke £60, Romsey £30 and Andover £50. There are frequent entries in the town accounts for payment of Ship Money, e.g. "pd. 10sh. for 3 months tax for ye shipping money."

ESCAPE TO A NEW ENGLAND

Politics, religion and a general dissatisfaction with the state of the country led many non-conformists to look for a new home. America, in the shape of New England appeared to them the most likely prospect, a large, virtually unexplored land, an ideal place to practise their own beliefs away from the restrictions imposed by the King and by Archbishop Laud. Between 1620 and 1642 nearly 80,000 people left these shores for the harsh realities of New England. They included Peter Noyes, a Puritan churchwarden of Weyhill church who, having borrowed £80, led a party from the Andover area to Waterdown, Massachusetts in the ship *Confidence*, sailing from Southampton. He took with him his eldest son and daughter, his neighbour John Bent and three servants. Liking what he saw, Noyes returned to Andover early in 1639 to dispose of his family affairs and gathered together eleven other inhabitants of Weyhill, paying a total of £76. 8s. 0d on 12 April, 1639 for their passage on the ship *Jonathan* to New England. Noyes later went on to co-found the community of Sudbury, and become a Commissioner for the government of Massachusetts, and a Church Elder as well as Town Deputy to the Massachusetts Legislature. He died in 1657.

Undoubtedly others from the Andover district left for the New World and perhaps founded many of the twenty or so other 'Andovers' scattered all over the American states and more exist in Canada and Tasmania.

THE CIVIL WAR

Upon the resumption of Parliament in April 1640, two MPs were elected for Andover, Sir Richard Wynn and Robert Wallop, but because the king was refused his demands it was quickly dissolved and became later known as the Short Parliament. However, Charles realised later that year that it was necessary to recall Parliament, when he found it impossible to obtain funds from elsewhere to finance his fight with the Scottish rebels. Robert Wallop was once again chosen to represent Andover, his partner this time being Sir Henry Rainsford.

Sir Henry was not able to serve long, for in March 1641 he contracted smallpox and was dead by the end of the month. In a new election Mr Harry Vernon, a Royalist and relation of Robert Wallop, was elected for Andover but the defeated candidate, Sir William Waller, disputed the va-

28. Sir William Waller, declared Andover's MP in May 1642, after a disputed election with Harry Vernon.

lidity of the result. He submitted a petition to Parliament claiming Vernon's seat, but the case was not heard until a year later. A report was made to the House that showed the right of election of an MP for Andover lay with the 24 Burgesses of the town. On this particular occasion it was found that 18 were present, and that their vote was evenly split between the two candidates. The casting vote for Mr Vernon was made by the Bailiff. The report also noted that three other burgesses were prevented from voting, as they had not taken their oath, one of whom was a declared Waller supporter.

In the House of Commons Journal it is reported that "Mr Vernon's Election to serve as Burgess in this Parliament, for the town of Andever is void". A vote was called to decide if Sir William Waller's election was good and the votes were 107 to 102 in his favour, whereupon they declared Waller the MP for Andover. He took up his seat on 12 May 1642, together with his other duties in the Parliamentary Army.

SEQUESTRATION OF ARMS

Civil War seemed ever more inevitable in 1642. Locally, Parliament ordered the Hampshire local gentry to sequester any arms, ammunition, money or other provisions from those suspected of making war against them. William Blake, William Jervis and William Cooper, prominent Andover residents, were among the Royalists targeted.

EJECTION OF ANDOVER'S VICAR

Meanwhile, religious discord had heightened. In 1641 an Act was passed stating that "…. it shall be lawful for the parishioners of any parish … to set up a lecture, and to maintain an orthodox minister at their own charge to preach every Lord's Day where there is no preaching, and to preach one day in every weekly lecture.' Where parishes did not take advantage of this order the House of Commons stepped in to insist that ministers allow the lecturers the free use of their pulpits. The law was passed mainly to mute the Laudian ministers, and also to take away the congregations from the disenfranchised, so-called 'mechanick preachers', who believed that the holy spirit was within them, and who were accused of subverting the moral standards of society.

This Act had serious repercussions in Andover. First reports of the 'infamous' exploits of the Revd Robert Clark, Vicar of Andover, are to be found in the House of Commons Journal for the year 1642.

> August 12, 1642. Whereas information was this day given to the House that Mr Clarke, vicar of Andover doth obstinately refuse to obey the order of this House in admitting of Mr Symonds to preach there as Lecturer, and gives out that he his wife and children will all be put to death before they condescend to the said order."

Clark was cited for contempt of Parliament and summoned to appear again on 24 August, when witnesses were called and testified that he had given a command to lock the church doors. The vicar was alleged to have said rather than that Mr Symonds should preach there by order of Parliament he would lose his life, and his wife and children should die in prison; that the church was as much his own as his own house, and he "would hold his right to let the Parliament do what they would." The witnesses' information was firmly denied, and Clark was asked to withdraw. When recalled the Speaker of the House informed him that they were not satisfied with his answer, and that the witnesses' statements had been proved. He was then committed to the King's Bench prison, during the pleasure of the House and the Lecturer, Mr Symonds, was allowed to take his position at Andover. The Vicar's resolution soon wilted, however:

> Thursday, September 1, 1642, ordered, that Mr Robert Clark, upon his humble petition, expressing his sorrow that he had offended the House, be forthwith discharged from any further imprisonment.

But this was not the end of his opposition to the Lecturer. He suffered a great deal of humiliation by harassment and his house was plundered and defaced. His books were stolen and those not taken were 'torn to pieces'. In defiance of the order to stop preaching, Clark was later forced to convey himself through a hole in the top of his house, lowering himself by a rope into the adjoining tenement. On one occasion he was assaulted in the church, and ran home, narrowly escaping a rain of bullets the local soldiery fired at him. He was forced eventually to leave town, a shower of stones and abuse making the journey more uncomfortable.

During the period when Andover was without a permanent minister, the Parliamentary Committee put the management of the services in the hands of a blacksmith named Leggat and a brazier by the name of Butcher, who in turn put a lock on the door of the pulpit to keep out 'undesirable' preachers.

The people of Andover protested to the Corporation, asking them to provide a competent minister. The Corporation took up the case with the patrons of the church. St Mary's College, Winchester, which appointed a Mr Millett, a curate of Aldbourne, Wiltshire as minister.

On the restoration of Charles II, the exiled Robert Clark returned to Andover from Northleach in Gloucestershire, where he had been appointed vicar. He travelled down on Saturday, incognito, spending the night at the house of a friend. On the Sunday morning he entered the church, where there was a full congregation and ousted Mr Millett, telling him "Sir, the King has come to his own and will reign alone, and I am come to my own and will officiate without an Assistant." He then continued with the service giving a sermon on the 'Forgiving of Injuries' to the satisfaction of the congregation.

DECLARATION OF WAR

In August 1642 the King raised his standard at Nottingham and the English Civil War began. To pay for it Parliament imposed new taxes. One in particular was the 'assessment and excise tax', introduced by John Pym in 1643. This was really a land and property tax, modelled on Ship Money, levied on the 'true yearly value of rent, annuities and offices'. Previously the taxes had fallen on merchants and the smaller man of property, but now the tables were turned and it was the landed classes who bore the brunt of them. This tax was certainly not one-sided though for it also taxed the poor, who had to pay duties on most articles of popular consumption. e.g. beer, meat, salt, soap and paper. After the Restoration the tax was confined to luxury items, beer and spirits, cider, tea, coffee and chocolate.

William Blake, a prominent member of Andover Corporation, and a linen draper, was caught up in this, for in 1648 he was ordered to pay a fine or composition of two years income ".... the value of the site to be reckoned as it stood before the civil war broke out", under the Land Assessment Act.

AFTER THE BATTLE OF CHERITON

The Battle of Cheriton on 29 March 1644 dId not go well for the Royalists and they were forced to retreat. Colonel Sir John Smith was badly wounded on the battlefield and after being rescued by his troop, retired to Wonston, a village about five miles north of Winchester. By morning it was realised the Colonel's condition was weakening and they resolved to attempt to take him to the relative safety of Oxford. Eyewitness to the event, Edward Walsingham, relates:

> When we drew neare Andover he began to say (his senses being a little astonished) 'Good my Lord let us charge them once again and the day is ours.' As soon as we entered the towne he began to invoke the sacred name of Jesus often repeating it with a gust and sweetnesse in the divine vertue of it.
>
> Shortly after, over and against the signe of the Angel, in a mild repose he expired where it would have grieved the hardest heart to have seen him round enclosed with sundry gentlemen, condoling with teares the untimely end of so Feerelesse a Gentleman.

Smith's body was later given a stately burial at Oxford on 1 April 1644.

ORDERED INTO THE WEST

After the Parliamentary successes at Oxford, the Lord General, the Earl of Essex and Sir William Waller discussed the best way of completing the King's discomfiture. Waller reluctantly stayed in the Midlands and followed the retreating King. Essex, perhaps a little jealous of Waller's recent successes, marched westward with the idea of relieving the besieged town of Lyme Regis, hoping to cut off the Queen and her forces at Exeter. Essex had barely set foot toward Lyme when he received letters from Waller urging him back, where with his help he could settle with the King in a couple of days. Essex ignored Waller's letter and continued the march, leaving Waller to his own devices.

The King now gathered fresh breath, collecting new recruits and provisions and turned as if to march on Oxford. His forces met those of Waller at Cropedy Bridge, and inflicted heavy losses on them. With little now to stop him now joining his wife at Exeter, the King marched into the West and by 18 August 1644 it was reported to the Committee of Both Kingdoms that the Lord General was in difficulties, surrounded by four armies.

Waller was ordered into the West with as much of an army as he could muster. Sir William set off on 7 September with only 2000 foot, 800 horse and 150 dragoons, but even with such a small army he was able to effect a unification of the two armies at Lostwithiel. Waller and his troops remained in Wiltshire and Dorset strengthening the south coast garrisons, but despite all the new recruits he was gathering he still had not enough men to attack the King and urged the Committee to send more. Fearing the King would break through and attack Oxford the Committee ordered the Earl of Manchester to Oxford to fill the gap left by Waller's march westward.

Manchester was slow to comply and on 27th September his army still lingered in Middlesex. The Committee urged Manchester to send his cavalry ahead to join Waller and Essex at Shaftesbury and his foot regiment was to rendezvous with Essex's re-equipped infantry at Newbury. Manchester was slow in complying for he was still at Reading during mid October and it was not until the King's army was at the Hampshire border that he marched to join the army of the Earl of Essex.

THE BATTLE OF ANDOVER

Waller fell back toward the combined armies of Essex and Manchester. After marching through Salisbury, Waller ordered his 3,000 cavalry and 1,500 dragoons to halt at Winterborne Stoke, near Amesbury, where he was on 15 October when he heard that the King's army was nearing Salisbury. Sir William immediately fell back to Andover, still a considerable distance in advance of the combined armies.

In Salisbury the King hatched plans to attack Waller at Andover. At seven o'clock in the morning of 18 October 1644 his army mustered at Clarendon Park, although his foot soldiers did not arrive until eleven, delaying the march until noon that day. Despite the delay, the army came within four miles of Andover, near Monxton, before Waller had any indication of its whereabouts. Sir William's response was to muster his

29. *An account of the Battle of Andover, from the Mercurius Aulicus, 1644.*

MERCVRIVS AVLICVS,

Communicating the Intelligence and affaires of the Court, to the rest of the KINGDOME.

The 42 VVeeke, ending Octob. 19. 1644.

His Majesty staid at *Salisbury* Tuesday night, Wednesday, & Thursday, and on Friday advanced towards *Andover* in *Hampshire* where the Rebells lay, with intention to stoppe His Majesties motion ; somewhat short of *Andover* a Forelorne hope being sent out, met with another of the Rebells very neare their maine body; both charged & kept their ground, till two bodies of His Majesties Horse came up and marched into the field, where the Rebells stood ; at sight whereof the Rebells forces began to fly out at the other end of *Andover* Towne ; yet made not so good speed, but that His Majesties horse overtooke them, and slashed them soundly, especially in a Lane entring into the Towne, where that body of Rebells was routed, and very good execution done upon them, pursuing them through *Andover* a good way beyond, till the darke night stept further persuit. Which done, His Majesty marched into *Andover* and lay there all night: This Morning He advanced towards *Whitechurch*, and sent the Earle of Northampton with his owne Bragade of horse to visit Master *John Fines* at the siege of *Banbury* Castle, where Sir *William Compton* (his Lordships Brother) hath so handsomly entertained Col. *Fines*, that upon the gallant Earles approach M' *Fines* will follow his own Fathers example but not his instructions, as you shall heare next Weeke under his Fathers owne hand.

FINIS.

army on the outskirts of Andover as if he meant to fight. Upon sight of the huge army the King was commanding, Waller withdrew through the town leaving behind a strong party of horse and dragoons to cover his retreat.

Seeing this the King's troops charged and "routed them with good execution, and pursued them through the town, and slew many of them in the rear, until the darkness of the night secured them and hindered the others from following farther". Fighting lasted around two hours, by which time about 80 prisoners were taken in an area covering two miles. Among the prisoners was William Carr, a colonel in Waller's army. Another was a captain, "a Scot, that died, who a little before his death rose from under the table, saying he would not die like a dog under the table, but sat down on the chair and immediately died of his wounds".

The battle is said to have taken place in a lane leading into Andover, in the region of Red Post Bridge and indeed a few pieces of cannonball and musketballs have been discovered in the area near Upper Mill Farm, Monxton. About thirty of Waller's men were killed and about ten to twenty of the King's (although there is some ambiguity of figures between the chroniclers).

The King quartered for the night at the White Hart Inn, now known as the Danebury Hotel. The next day his army marched to relieve the besieged at Donnington Castle at Newbury, stopping briefly at Whitchurch.

There are several references made to the battle of Andover in the town records, especially those of the burial of soldiers, generally from the inns, viz. "a stranger from ye plow" (now the Southampton Arms, "Ye Starr" (now the White Hart Hotel), etc. Although Waller made only a fleeting visit to the town it found time to present him with a sugar loaf valued at 13s. 4d.

UNREST IN THE RANKS

For a short period around the end of 1645 a considerable number of soldiers were being quartered in the area as a troop was raised in readiness for service in Ireland. The long wait to raise a satisfactory number of soldiers made the men restless and more so when the pay fell into arrears. One report from Upper Clatford suggested that the men had decided between themselves that the Irish expedition was out of the question and they hoped for a resurgence of Royalist activity in the area to keep them busy.

The restlessness grew into mutiny and they began stealing and robbing to make ends meet. One of the official collectors of sequestrations for the Andover district, Gabriel Floyd, while on his way to Longparish to meet the senior collector, John Marks, was seized and plundered by a troop of horse under the command of Major Gifford. Marks went to investigate and, according to his own testimony, was called a rogue by the major, robbed of his linen, money and other items and detained for half an hour.

Robbing and stealing continued and it was said that the disgruntled soldiers also took money from people as they left the fair at Collingborne. The County Committee wrote to Speaker Lenthall on 5 December 1645 to complain and begged for relief. It took Parliament almost six weeks to put matters right, providing about £1750 to aid the speedy despatch of Jephson's regiment to Ireland. The men were still reluctant to go and the Committee of Both Kingdoms was still urging Col. Jephson 'to expedite matters' in February the following year.

ANOTHER FIRE IN ANDOVER

In 1647, a fire consumed the greater part of the west side of the Upper High Street, rendering 82 families homeless. It is thought that the west side from the Guildhall up to where 'Baldocks' was (69/71 High Street) was destroyed right back to the river. Winchester College, which owned most ot the property burnt down, granted the grand total of £5 to cover the losses of all 82 families, but to one man Robert Mountain who lost property valued at £800 they granted £1. The town's Charity Chamberlains also deemed it necessary to relieve the stricken by granting the sum of £10 towards their losses.

The fire remained heavily on the minds of the townsfolk for many years afterward and there were many cases brought before the town's courts "for making a fier agaynst a Chimney or Flew, which is very dangerous". In 1650 the Corporation ordered that "none shall thatch any house or howses in or next to the high streete in Andever". Similarly in 1668 the Corporation ordered the removal to the river of the kilns used by leather tanners, as it was felt they constituted a danger to the town.

THE LEVELLERS

By 1649 the Leveller movement had infiltrated the army and attempted to dissuade soldiers from fighting in a forthcoming Irish Expedition. Due to their influence and a lack of pay many men mutinied to form a regiment opposed to the views of Parliament. Oliver Cromwell was sent to quash this small band and arrived in Andover on 12 May, 1649 where he addressed each of the regiments, appealing to them in the name of unity and discipline and their past services together.

> That he was resolved to live and die with them, and that as he had often engaged *with* them against the common enemy of this nation, so he resolved still to persist therein, against those revolters which are called by the name of Levellers; not doubting but that they would as one man unite, and with unanimous spirit follow him, for the subduing of them, and bringing in the Ring-leaders thereof to exemplary punishment.

Eventually the rebellious soldiers were caught at Burford and routed.

During his very short stay during this incident Sir Thomas Fairfax, the Lord General, was presented with a sugar loaf as the Town accounts witness:

> payd. Benia Bradborne May the 12th 1649 for a sugar loafe given to the Lord General 0—16s 0d."

Another important Parliamentarian, Judge Nicholas, who was made a Baron of the Exchequer during Cromwell's Protectorship, was in the town during 1650 and was treated to ... "a pottle of Sack' value 2s 8d when staying at the Angel Inn.

THE FALSE MESSIAH

In 1649, William Franklin, a ropemaker and native of Overton in Hampshire, but apprenticed and settled in London, was entangled in the religious fervour of these troubled times by pronouncing himself to be the Messiah. He said that he had been called "to go into the hill country, to the land of Ham" and he travelled from London by wagon and arrived at the Star Inn in Andover (now the

30. Sir Thomas Fairfax, from an engraving by H. Hondius.

White Hart Hotel) with his travelling companion, Mary Gadbury. Mary was honoured by Franklin with the title of 'the spouse of Christ, the Lamb's wife'.

In a very short time, Franklin involved many locals in his ravings. Goody Waterman of Clanville was proclaimed the 'King's daughter, all glorious within', with John Noyes of Nutbane as John the Baptist, whose duty was to pronounce the coming of the false prophet into the world; Edward Spradbury of Andover was given the title of 'reconciling angel' and Henry Dixon, the 'destroying angel'.

The authorities eventually decided to take action and the chief actors were arrested and tried at the Winchester Spring Sessions in 1650. Franklin, rather tamely abandoned his claim to be Christ and was given a long period of imprisonment. Mary Gadbury, indignant at Franklin's betrayal, suffered the additional humiliation of being flogged; others were bound over to be of good behaviour.

Interregnum and Restoration

THE PENRUDDOCK UPRISING

After the execution of Charles I in 1649 and during the Interregnum, several men from the Andover area were arrested after a failed uprising in the West planned by Col. John Penruddock and Sir John Wagstaffe. Most of the members of the Royalist 'Sealed Knot' movement and some leading Presbyterians, who had promised their services, changed their minds at the last minute and from that moment the rebellion was doomed. On 11 March 1655 a group of about one hundred Royalists, including some Levellers, together with Penruddock and Wagstaffe, met at Clarendon Park near Salisbury from whence they marched on to Blandford. Here some eighty more men joined them. They marched back toward Salisbury, where just outside the city they were met by a small contingent from the Andover area. The group, now some two hundred strong, entered Salisbury.

They placed a strong guard on the city, rounded up all the available horses and collected a good few new recruits, many from the prisoners held in the town gaol. The Assizes were meeting in the town and the group apprehended numerous important judges. They rode out of the city back toward Blandford expecting to be met by the troops of Sir William Waller and Lord Fairfax, but unknown to Penruddock's men they had declined to turn out. Central government dispatched a formidable force to quash the uprising and within a short space of time Penruddock was captured, his force fighting on gallantly for three to four hours before being crushed.

Among prisoners from the Andover area were:

Richard Reeves, of Kimpton, gent. (mentioned as a Lt. Col.)
Thomas Helliard, of Upton, gent.
Edward Moreing, of Andover, weaver
Joseph Moreing, of Andover, yeoman
Robert Browne, of Andover, Cordwainer
Edward Painter, of Andover, Currier
Richard Miles (or Mills), of Andover, clothworker
Richard Hyard, of Amport, husbandman
Richard Goleston, of Amport, gent.
Leonard Catkill, of Cholderton, waggoner

John Williams, of Pyfield, carter
William Lewington, of Linkenholt, husbandman

Richard Reeves and Thomas Helliard were hanged at Exeter but the fate of the others is more obscure, although it was a ruling at the trials that some should be transported to Barbados in the West Indies.

One Andover trader disadvantaged by the Penruddock uprising was Peter Blake, a prominent member of the town council and businessman, who had supplied goods valued at over £75 to a certain John Lucas, who had been executed for his part in the rebellion. Blake applied to Cromwell for satisfaction out of Lucas's estate.

THE FIRST QUAKER IN ANDOVER

Further religious persecution occurred in Andover, when on 16 February 1658, Humphrey Smith, the first Quaker to preach in the town, was arrested. Judge Wyndham committed him to Winchester Gaol until he would give security for his good behaviour and there he remained until after March 1659, during which time he wrote several books and pamphlets.

For the second Parliament under the Protectorate, Andover found it unnecessary to return a member, although two were appointed for the short session under Richard Cromwell. On the 4 January, 1659 Gabriel Beck of the City of Westminster and Robert Gough of Vernham's Dean, were returned as MPs for Andover.

THE NEW STREET BARN CASE

New legislation after the Restoration in 1660 clamped down on non-conformists. In 1662, the Act of Uniformity required ministers of the Church of England to sign the Thirty-Nine Articles, or resign from it. Mr Samuel Sprint, a minister at nearby South Tidworth felt unable to conform to the liturgy of the Established Church and in 1662 he retired to Clatford. The Conventicle Act of 1664 established a scale of fines for those attending non-conformist services within five miles of a corporate town.

In his book *Historical Memorials of a Christian Fellowship*, J.S. Pearsall writes that :

. . . a group of eminent Christians residing at Andover ... frequently held a prayer meeting, at a distance of four miles from the town. To escape detection, they left their homes by moonlight, and selected for their Bethel, a dell in the quiet recesses of a wood.

DON QUIXOT Redivivus

Encountring A

BARNS·DOOR

OR AN

Exact Narrative

OF THE

RARE EXPLOITS

Of Captain *Braines* in a Dangerous
Expedition against a Certain BARN in
a Town on the other Side of the River ЯDDE
in the Land of *Little Ease*, and *Less Forbear*

UNDER THE COMMAND

Of *Tom Coxcomb* Signifer, an Over-grown Tap-
ster, and Principle-Member of the Disloyal Society of
the *Vitiosi*, and of the Corruption of the said
Town, and Sometime a Justice of the
Peace there.

Printed for the Company of INFORMERS

31. *Don Quixote Redivivus – a contemporary account of the New Street Barn Case, 1664.*

For a time no-one took much notice and the non-conformist sect grew bolder, meeting in a barn in New Street, Andover, under the leadership of Sprint and Dr Isaac Chauncy. But on 10 August 1673 an event which became known as 'The New Street Barn Case' occurred. Acting on information supplied by Robert Mooring and Solomon Hunt they fined Chauncy £20 for preaching, fourteen attenders five shillings each and Richard Ventham and Phillip Barnard £20 together for allowing the meeting in their barn. At the same time they fined Richard Butcher, one of the Constables of Andover, £5 for being present at the meeting and exercising religion in other manner than is allowed by the 'Littugis' and for omitting to inform the Justices.

On 7 September, members of the local militia led by Thomas Westcombe, a local Justice of the Peace, mingled with the congregation and when Samuel Sprint began to preach they rose to their feet ordering the meeting to cease. Sprint refused saying they had no warrant, whereupon Thomas Westcombe left the barn, going to St Mary's churchyard, where according to a contemporary account, *Don Quixot Redivivus Encountering a Barns Door,* he wrote out a warrant upon a tomb-stone commanding the local militia to break up the

meeting. The two preachers, Sprint and Chauncy were taken into custody and held for the night at the White Swan Inn, where Westcombe was landlord.

On the following Monday morning the justices imposed 5 shilling fines on another seventeen first offenders, Richard Ventham and Phillip Barnard were once again jointly fined £20 and there were 10 shilling fines on ten, second time offenders. No official record has survived to show Dr Chauncy's punishment but according to a contemporary account, which contains numerous errors, he was fined £20 for preaching.

The local churchwardens refused to take sides in this farcical affair and were fined 5/- each for not taking action to suppress the meeting. Shortly afterwards, however, the non-conformists were granted a licence to preach and moved to the upper floor of a pair of cottages in Sopers Lane (West Street) where it was converted into a chapel. The two preachers took turns there on alternate Sundays and when Mr Sprint preached it was a presbyterian ministry and when Dr Chauncy preached it was congregational.

Considerable friction occurred when attempting to unite the two non-conformist sects and after many reconciliation attempts the Congregationalists moved to a meeting house in Mark Lane under their minister Dr Isaac Watts.

THE WEYHILL FAIR DISPUTE BEGINS

No-one knows when Weyhill Fair began – it was ancient in the fourteenth century when Ramridge Manor, on whose land part of the fair was held, was granted to the Hospital of Ewelme in Oxfordshire. The grant of Weyhill Fair to the Corporation of Andover had been contentious (*see p34*). Rumblings of the dispute continued into the time of the Commonwealth, as is evidenced by two documents in Queen's College, Oxford. One notes that:

> Despite receiving annually £20-£30 in dues from the fair, the Andover men attempted on various occasions in James [I's] time and in the Commonwealth to move the fair. They chose Richard Cromwell as their High Steward.

The other states:

> If the town of Andover insist upon their loyalty & reflections be made on Mr. Drake or his predecessors, it may be replyed, that the first

The CASE of Ewelm Hofpital, Appellants, in Relation to Wayhil-Fair, againft the Corporation of Andover.

THAT *William De La Pool*, Duke of *Suffolk*, being heretofore feized of the Mannor of *Ramridge* in *Hampfhire*, did in King *Henry* the Sixth's time, by Licenfe Found the Hofpital of *Ewelm* in *Oxfordfhire*, which he appointed to confift of a Mafter, School-Mafter, and Thirteen poor Men, and Endowed it with the faid Mannor of *Ramridge*, and other Lands, referring only to himfelf the Nomination of the faid Mafter, *&c.*

That *Wayhil*-Fair (being a Fair by Prefcription) has been held time out of mind about *Michaelmas*-Day on part of the faid Mannor called *Ramridge-Down*, and fome part of it on a place called *Bliffomer-Hall-Acre*, and the reft of the Fair on the Glebe of the Rectory of *Wayhil*, the Advowfon whereof was given to *Queens-College*, *Oxon* by King *Charles* the Firft, and the Incumbents thereof have ever fince the Twenty Sixth of *Henry* the Eighth, paid Forty Shillings to the Crown in the Firft-Fruits for the cafual Profits of Standing of the Fair, which of late Years have been worth to the Incumbent Sixty Pounds a Year.

That ever fince the *Hofpital* had the Mannor, they or their Tenants have yearly received about One Hundred and Twenty Pounds for the Pickage and Stallage for Stalls, Booths, Penns and Hurdles for Sheep in the faid Fair, which has been the chief Support of the *Hofpital* by Fines, on granting Leafes and great Rents.

That the Corporation of *Andover*, obferving that no Toll or Show-Money was paid for Goods, Cattle, or Sheep fold therein, did in the One and Fortieth Year of Queen *Elizabeth* procure a Grant to them of the Fair at *Wayhil*, with a Court of *Pye-Powder*, and Licenfe to take Toll, Show-Money, and other ufual Perquifites of a Fair, and they got inferted in their Grant likewife the Profits of Pickage and Stallage.

That after this Grant the Fair was always held in the fame place as formerly, and the Corporation of *Andover* did never pretend to any thing more than to the Care and Government of the Fair, and the Toll and the above-mentioned Perquifites.

But the Pickage and Stallage was always paid to the *Hofpital* or their Tenants for breaking the Ground, *&c.* as Owners of the Soil, the Corporation having no Land there, whereby to have any fuch Pickage and Stallage.

That the Corporation of *Andover*, obferving the Advantages of Pickage and Stallage to be fo confiderable, did by their Intereft in 1683. procure a New Charter,

32. The Weyhill Fair Dispute. 'The Case of Ewelm Hospital' dated 1678 in which the Bailiffs of Andover attempted to move the fairground on to land they owned nearer the town.

time they refused to pay for their standings on Weyhill to the farmer of Ramridge was in the times of the usurpation, or in about the years [16]54 and 55: that in those times they put up Oliver's armie in the church & chose Richard Cromwell for their high steward, in expectation (tis said) to get Weyhill fair therby, & they had so great hopes of it then that they bought a piece of ground, called the hundred acres, about midway between Weyhill and Andover, to place it on.

Both these documents suggest that Andover had begun to assert its claim to the fair with tenacity and determination. Richard Cromwell's election to the High Stewardship of Andover was an obvious ploy to obtain Parliament's sympathy to their cause.

The businessmen of Andover saw the fair as a great market for their wares and realised its potential, especially if it could be restricted to land over which they held rights. They could then secure for themselves the substantial benefits arising from piccage and stallage. (These were rents derived from the fair – piccage was income from providing fodder for the animals, and stallage was derived from the pens for sheep and cattle.) They already had such rights upon lands that they rented but had to share profits with other landowners. In an effort to secure the profits, the bailiff and burgesses of Andover petitioned

the King for a new charter with several new grants and privileges asking that the fair be removed to land over which Andover had jurisdiction.

Mr Drake of Ewelme Hospital and a Mr Sanderson jointly opposed the petition and counter-petitioned the Lord Chancellor. A caveat was issued in September 1672, requiring that no grant should be made to hold a fair near Andover to the prejudice of Weyhill, and that the Weyhill Fair should not be removed to Andover. This however had little effect for the next year the Men of Andover made a disturbance endeavouring to move it from the hospital lands. The King was asked to intervene and an Order in Council was obtained to keep the fair on its original site. Still the Men of Andover came back, forcing the Hospital of Ewelme, William Drake their tenant, and Constance his wife, to bring an action at law, which was decided in the hospital's favour on 26 July 1674.

Both sides became determined in their endeavours. Lawsuits multiplied and Andover found it necessary to borrow money in order to continue with theirs. In 1682 the borough decided that the loans should be repaid out of the profits from the fair, should they win the case.

The King, since the Restoration, was anxious to exercise a strict control over the borough towns, in order that he could secure the election of Members of Parliament sympathetic to his own interests and policies. To this end he had insti-

33. *The Great Sheep Fair at Weyhill, c.1900, held on the downs at Weyhill near to the church.*

tuted a thorough investigation of borough franchises and charters throughout the country.

Andover townsmen saw this as an opportunity to obtain a new charter tailored to suit their present needs. The services of Sir Robert Sawyer, Attorney General, were obtained and by November 1682 the King and his Council discussed the matter. The King granted the new Charter but added the stipulation that he reserved the authority to nominate and declare the removal of the Steward or his deputy and the Town Clerk of the borough.

Andover Corporation accepted the new provision and nominations, and set about putting their new-found regulations into use. The part of the Charter most important to the Corporation was that dealing with the siting of the fair and was said in very few words:

> ..... to begin the day before the feast of St Michael and to be held at Wayhill within the Hundred of Andover in such convenient place as the Bailiff, Steward and two other Justices of the Peace of the Borough shall appoint"

on the three parcells of ground. viz., on the lands belonging to the Manor of Ramridge, Blissomer Hall acre and the Glebe lands. And therefore doe thinke fitt and so order and decree that the said faire be for the future be kept by the Bailiffe, Approved men and Burgesses of Andover on the said 3 places according to the said verdict. And that Andevor be enjoined from keeping the said faire from the lands mentioned in the said verdict for the future.

Andover was still determined in its efforts and obtained a new trial. A Middlesex Jury in 1686 found for the borough, with the Court ordering that the profits of the previous three years be paid to the town.

Once again the Hospital appealed and the Lord Chancellor ordered Sir Robert Sawyer, the Attorney-General, to mediate. Representatives of both parties met at his house at Highclere, hopefully to iron out any difficulties and come to a happy conclusion. What was agreed at the meeting is told below:

> Note yt on tewsday 10 Aug., 66, Mr. Attorney-Generall in ye presence of severall members of Andever Corporacon, and of Dr. Dixon, Rector of Wayhill, proposed an accomodacon an yt Andover should be Kynde to ye church, and should give him for use of his glebe 20li per ann. duringe faire at Wayhill, and remitt ye 3 last years profitts and his part of ye costs, ye Dr. craved tyme to consider of it till tewsday then next following, at whch tyme he declared yt he would not assent thereto unlesse Andever would give him 10li per ann. more.

Dr Dixon later agreed to accept a rent from Andover Corporation for the Glebe lands of £35 per annum and that year the Andover Corporation removed the fair to Cholderton.

Just when it was thought that the whole matter was at a close, in 1690 Mr Drake initiated a Bill of Review which resulted in a fourth trial at King's Bench. This time a Hampshire jury found for Drake and a Decree was issued according to the Court's verdict. The town, angered by this decision, petitioned the Commisioners, who ordered that Ewelme should not set up pens on their own land. Andover then obtained secret leases of the glebe and Blissimere Hall Acre and set up the most profitable part of the fair there.

Ewelme finally took the matter to the House of Lords who on 4 February 1693 reversed the Decree of 22 Sept 1692.

The fair was then moved to ground belonging to the town at East Cholderton, securing for Andover the substantial profits arising from it.

The Master of the hospital and his tenants were prepared to fight the matter to the bitter end and again went to court, obtaining a verdict both at the assizes and at the Exchequer from Hampshire juries. They also obtained decrees in Chancery, the last stating:

> The Court on hearing the whole matter and what could be aleadged on either side and reading the last verdict for keeping the said faire

MISUSE OF THE CHARITY FUND

During the early months of 1692 rumour spread around Andover that the 'Charitable Uses' fund was being used to pay the legal costs of the Weyhill Fair dispute. The Bailiff ordered an inspection to be made of the charity funds and written down in order that:

> .. all persons may be satisfyed how that affair stands that the toewn and publique Officers may be freed of the scandall throwne upon them by ill men.

Two weeks later it was further ordered:

> ... that an Inspection be made into all the Charities of this towne and that Notice be tymely & publeqly given to all persons that will meet this day sennight to heare all complaynts & receyve any informacons of any miscarriages in or about the said Charities.

On 14 August one irate Andover inhabitant, William Hayward, fixed notices to the west door of St Mary's church and to the door of the Independent chapel in Sopers Lane. On these notices he listed the lands and rents paid to the Corporation and those that should have been devoted to the relief of the poor.

He was arrested, publicly examined and then punished for his 'misdemeanours' by being whipped from the town gaol in Bridge Street to the gate of the Angel Inn at the top of the High Street.

A short while later the Corporation placed a wooden board in the church on which they listed all the benefactions which had been made to the Corporation. Numerous mistakes were made during its preparation, showing the haste in which it was prepared.

Could there have been a cover up? Was the money being used to finance the Weyhill Fair proceedings? It must be said that the speed with which the 'Benefactions Tablet' was erected does suggest so, but no real evidence exists to prove it beyond doubt.

The irony of this tale comes when some eight years later the very persons who were so quick to condemn Hayward, citing him as a liar, were themselves taken into custody and charged with

34. William Hayward was sentenced to be whipped from the town gaol in Bridge Street to the gate of the Angel Inn at the top of the High Street – from 'Whipping a Vagrant' in the Bagford Ballads.

the corruption of public affairs. The Bailiff, Julius Samborne, and the town's two justices of the peace, Edward Warham and Joseph Wimbleton, were brought betore the House of Lords to answer the charges, but when found guilty were sent to the Tower of London for the night after which they were reprimanded on their knees and then discharged – a much lighter punishment than the indignity poor old Hayward suffered.

TRADE TOKENS

The Civil War caused a serious shortage of small coinage, which still pertained after the Restoration. In many towns, including Andover, traders and town officials tried to alleviate this by issuing their own money, known as tokens, struck in base metals. The town's pieces bore the legend 'For ye poores benefit' and featured a cripple. Each were valued at one farthing and dated from 1658 until 1666, when they also issued a halfpenny token.

A number of the town's more prominent businesses also issued tokens, all valued at one farthing except that of Richard Blake who issued one valued at a halfpenny and bore the arms of the Mercers' Company. This Blake was a former King's Waiter at Custom House, London and also a clothier and draper; he leased a corner shop under the Andover Guildhall in 1647 and was elected Bailiff in 1644/5. The use of copper and brass tokens was suppressed in 1672.

The Eighteenth Century

AN END TO DISPUTED ELECTIONS?

A number of disputed elections for Andover's Members of Parliament ended in 1702 when Parliament decided that the right of election rested with the 'close' Corporation of twenty-four burgesses, and in spite of riots and disturbances this remained the rule. It was announced that an endeavour had been made at Andover 'corruptly to set to sale the election of a burgess' and the House of Commons resolved that it was unlawful to bribe a local authority to influence the election of members of Parliament.

PUTTING THE POOR TO WORK

In 1723 the government introduced a Workhouse Act empowering parishes to erect workhouses. In general, the poor were restricted to the workhouse building except on Sundays and vagrant children could be apprehended against the wishes of their parents. Poor people who refused to enter the workhouse could find themselves put out of the parish and were not entitled to relief.

The Churchwardens and Overseers for the Poor in Andover decided to lease the Plough Inn in Winchester Street (now the site of the Southampton Arms), for their workhouse. The property was owned by Dorothy Baker, a widow, who let it for an annual rent of 5 guineas for a period of 14 years for the "lodging, keeping, maintaining and employing the poor". An agreement was struck with Thomas Noyes, a shalloon maker, to employ all persons capable of working for the next three years. (A shalloon was a kind of light woollen cloth used for coat linings and for women's dresses.)

Noyes was required to supply the wool and yarn that were required whilst the Churchwardens and Overseers were to provide the looms, furniture for the workhouse and other utensils. Noyes was also required to ensure that the inmates were decently clothed and fed and that a matron was employed to live in and look after them. For his part of the contract Noyes was paid £10 per annum but in addition he was able to purchase the finished cloths at a generous 25% discount.

Orders for the regulation of the workhouse in 1737 make grim reading. Inmates were required to rise by 6am and go to bed at 9pm in the summer, and in the winter rise by 7am and go to bed by 8pm at the latest, excepting those who were required to work longer. The master and mistress appointed some of them to sweep and keep the place clean and wash clothes. The matron was to ensure everyone was kept clean, especially the children. Doors to the workhouse were kept locked at all times excepting Sundays when able bodied inmates were obliged to go to church.

Thomas Noyes' contract was not renewed and it was some fifteen months before Richard Willis, an apothecary, was appointed as the new Master. Benjamin Munday, another shalloon maker, provided the materials and took his profit but refused to be a Master. The last known lease for the workhouse is dated 1751 when William Walters, a serge weaver, and his wife were paid £20 a year to supervise it. No other information about this workhouse is known after this date.

A NEW GUILDHALL

An Andover Guildhall was built in 1725 to a design by Thomas Switzar, replacing an earlier building that had stood on the site since 1583. It was an imposing building of brick and Chilmark stone, with a Corinthian style portico housing a large sundial. There was a bell tower, topped by a weathervane and ball and the ground floor was open plan. A carpenter's bill exists for the work which describes the demolition of the old building and the erection of the new in great detail. The carpenter was Alexander Banks, who was paid £46. A further bill for work done in 1725 also exists:

"4 foot thic light sash glass £2 3 0
Laying 5 tun 10 hundred lead ready cast at Is.
per hundred £5 10 0
281b. Leader at 9d. per lb. £1 1 0
8 foot of Quarry glass £0 4 0
40 foot of Bristol Crown Glass for ye Councel
House at 10d. £1 13 4
8 windows London Crown do Is. per foot
£16 0 0
Samll. Hollis one lead weighed 12c lq 131
£12 7 4
Sarten Pipes 2c lq Ill £3 16 0
£42 14 8

(Quarry glass was a type of glass cut into diamond shapes and was used in lattice windows. Crown glass was made into sheets by the

35. Andover Guildhall, built in 1725 and demolished in 1825. It was designed by Thomas Switzar. From Warner's 'Hampshire'.

blowing, spinning and splitting technique; normally the thick centre part went into cottage windows.)

Throughout the life of the new building maintenance bills were a constant source for concern. In 1788, £242 needed to be spent on it, and then in 1820 an estimate for repairs came to £431. 3. 0d, which the Corporation deferred for four years. In 1824, a new, hastily prepared, survey of the 'Town Hall', as it was also known, was made and plans for a rebuilding were considered with the intention of preserving the form of the 'present front'.

In January 1825 the Town Clerk reported on plans of John Harris Langdon for construction of a new building in Bath stone. Thomas Ashetton Smith and Sir John Pollen, the MPs for Andover, were each to contribute £1000 towards its cost and there was to be a loan of £2000 at 5% from a Robert Sutton of London. The balance was to be made up from land sales at Andover Down and Picket Twenty.

During rebuilding the large front room at the Angel was used as a temporary Guildhall. Among the contractors were William Gibbs for stonework (£1600), William Lansley, carpenter (£1260), Joseph Turner, bricklayer (£355.17.0d), John Windover, slater (£57.10.0d), Robert Tasker, ironwork (£114.18.0d), William Herberts for plumbing and glazing and Mr Beare for painting. The final cost was around £7000.

The ground floor had an open plan format. What are now the large windows and main entrance doors were then merely arched openings giving access to an open space inside, where there were both shops and market stalls. The shops were known as 'The Shambles' – a name applied to purveyors of meat. It is not known when the butchers' shops were discontinued, but the Guildhall was used for some years on Friday mornings as a Corn Exchange. A photograph exists (*ill. 149*) of the scene at the Exchange *c.*1860 showing farmers in their frock coats and smocks. The Women's Institute nowadays makes use of the lower Guildhall for its weekly sales.

A SHAMELESS LIBERTINE

Sir Francis Blake Delaval, of Seaton Delaval in Northumberland and MP for Andover from 1754 to 1768, was the eldest of eight sons and three daughters of Capt. Francis Delaval. He married Lady Isabella Paulet, a widow, whom he married for her money. This paid for his numerous extra marital relationships until she caught him with one of his mistresses, Betty Le Roche, a young Ward of Court, whom he seduced while she was under the protection of his father's house at Seaton. A contemporary of the time called him "A shameless libertine and an impudent jackanapes".

Delaval's first encounter with Andover was in 1749 when he fought a by-election there, expecting to be elected by kissing a few babies and being charming to the voters' wives. He was mistaken, however and lost. Two years later he succeeded in gaining a seat in the House as MP for Hindon. At the next by-election in 1754 he returned to Andover to do battle. He had realised that the only way to get into Parliament was to bribe voters – his looks were not enough. He resorted to an election gimmick to attract votes. Shortly before the polling took place a culverin (a large cannon) was drawn into the market place, where Sir Francis announced he was going to load the barrel with some 500 gold sovereigns and fire it into the air. He won the seat, for in those days a sovereign was a fortnight's wage for a labourer.

The elections of 1761 nearly broke him however for he had to sell off some of the family silver

36. *Eastfield Road c.1905, a centre of the town's wool weaving industry for many years.*

37. *Rack Close, c.1905, where once the cloths were stretched on tenterhooks to dry.*

38. *The Round House at the junction of Salisbury and Weyhill Roads c.1900. A relic of the turnpike and coaching era, it was demolished in 1938 and its place was covered by a garden.*

to pay the bills. Delaval's lawyer and election agent, a man named Kelynge, arranged a dinner at the George Hotel and invited officers of a regiment camped near the town and the Mayor and Corporation of Andover. Each party was led to believe they were the guests of each other and when the time came to settle the bill found they were liable to pay their own bills. The colonel of the regiment was so angry he threw Kelynge out of the window, breaking both his legs. Kelynge later sued Sir Francis to the sum of £500.

NEW ROADS AND A CHANGING TOWN

The increase of road traffic in the eighteenth century made inevitable a better system for the maintenance of the main routes. Turnpike trusts were established by Acts of Parliament to do this. The Andover Trust, formed in 1755, took over the road from Basingstoke, through Worting, Overton, Whitchurch, Hurstbourne Priors, Andover, Middle Wallop to Lopscombe Corner on the Wiltshire border. Each of the Trust's 155 trustees swore on oath that he was a landowner worth £50 annual rent or in possession of £1500 in property. They were empowered to collect tolls at gates on three sections of the road. The tolls were set at 1 shilling for each coach or wagon; 1d for each riding horse; 10d per score of cattle or other large animal and 5d per score of small beasts, sheep, calves, pigs etc. Wagons with wheels wider than 9 inches could be charged at a lower rate.

The following year the road following the route of the present A30 between Basingstoke and Lopscombe Corner was also turnpiked.

An Andover landmark on the turnpike road, known as the Round House, stood at the junction of Weyhill Road and Salisbury Road in 1839. It was a hexagonal tollhouse built at the same time as another at the Railway Tavern crossroads. In 1854 General Shubrick, in commemoration of many happy years spent hunting in the area, presented to the town a clock "costing about £60", which was placed on the exterior of the Weyhill Road building for the benefit of travellers.

Turnpikes came to an end with the introduction of the Highways Act of 1861, but the turnpike gates were not removed until 1 November 1872. The clock was taken down at the same time and placed on the front of the Free Library in Bridge Street, now the Vine Trust bookshop and restaurant, where it remains to this day. However, the tollhouse itself was not demolished until October 1938.

During the latter part of the 18th century Andover was just beginning to emerge from a quiet agricultural and weaving town into one that businessmen considered ripe for expansion. The wool industry, which had been the backbone of its wealth for centuries, was in serious decline and something had to be found to replace it. George Ransom and Thomas Tarrant set up silk manufactories to take on redundant wool weavers.

The Turnpike roads improved communications

and Andover was an important staging post for coaches between London and the West Country, bringing prosperity to the older inns such as the Angel, Globe and Star and Garter (now the Danebury Hotel). New roads were planned linking Andover with London, Newbury, Devizes, Salisbury and Winchester, and by 1770 Andover was thought important enough for a projected canal linking it to the sea at Southampton.

All through this period, the great Weyhill Fair, held in October, was in the middle of a revival as a pleasure fair. The sheep fair was not so well attended as previously but could still boast around 50,000 sheep on the downs and the horse fair was famous for the sale of Irish hunters and Welsh ponies. Hops were a principal item on sale for the local brewing industry. The Revd Henry White, brother of the naturalist Gilbert White, was a frequent visitor to the fair at this time.

THE PEST HOUSE

Isolation was the recognised treatment for smallpox and other infectious diseases and so on 3 January 1757 Andover Corporation decided to erect a Pest House on the north side of London Lane, now known as Vigo Road. Two caretakers were employed, John and Eleanor Thorn, at a wage of 50/- a year and they were allowed to use the house and garden, which was surrounded by a chalk wall. The building remained until 1964 when it was demolished, the area where it once stood now being used for allotments.

COACHING DAYS

Sometime around 1750 a coaching incident with sinister overtones took place just outside the town. After travelling through severe snowstorms, the coach for Southampton arrived at Andover. Here the passengers alighted, refusing to go on. The coachman, a young and inexperienced man, insisted the coach was going on and drove off alone into the storm. The story, according to Margaret Baker, author of *Discovering the Westward Stage*, was that neither he or the coach and horses were ever seen again. "Locally it was thought he'd been carried off by the Devil". After the thaw, no sign of the coach could be found, until a hundred years later, when men digging in a peat bog near Dean, about 16 miles south of Andover, came across the skeleton of a man, four horses and fragments of the ironwork of a coach. Locals assumed these to be the remains of this mysterious incident.

Andover was an important staging area for coaches in all directions. The London to Exeter

39. Bridge Street around 1900. The large house on the left is Bishops Court House and on the right is Moore's Garage. The building in the foreground is Wharf House, the headquarters of the Andover Canal Company.

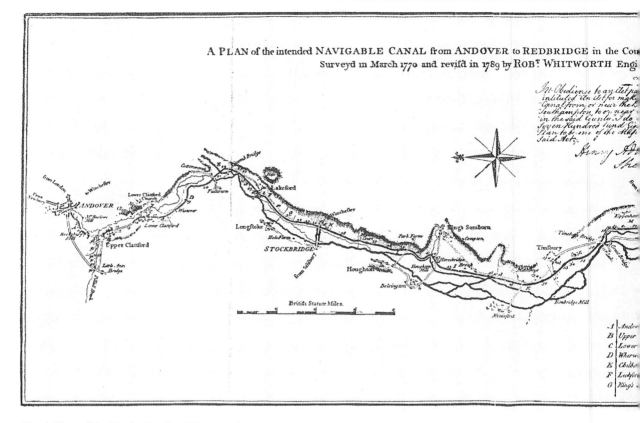

40. A Plan of the Navigable Canal from Andover to Redbridge, 1780, by Robert Whitworth, Engineer.

Royal Mail coach, via Salisbury, arrived at 5 in the morning at the Star and Garter Hotel and on the return trip it called in at 9.30pm en route via Hartford Bridge and Staines. The 'Exeter Balloon' coach also called at the Star and Garter on its inward and outward journeys.

Cooke's Salisbury to London coach called at the George Inn in the High Street at 7pm every day except Saturday, and at 5pm on the return journey, except Sunday. Yet another Salisbury coach, Steadman's 'Light Salisbury Coach' carried only four passengers to the Bull and Crown, Holborn. It called at the Bush Inn in Bridge Street on Monday, Wednesday and Friday at 7am and on the return journey on Tuesday, Thursday and Saturday at 3pm. There were in addition to the coaches a number of stage wagons, which carried merchandise of varying types that would also take passengers at the cheap rate of one shilling a day.

THE CANAL AGE

During the late 18th century the canal age began not with construction, but with little groups of promoters employing the few experienced engineers of the time to make surveys. One such survey was carried out by Robert Whitworth, one of the foremost canal engineers of his time, during 1770 when he surveyed the valleys of the Anton and Test rivers to estimate the possibility of a canal to link the towns of Andover and Southampton.

He estimated that a narrow canal could be built at a cost of £28,982 and a bigger one at £31,654. Meetings in support of such a project were held at Andover, Stockbridge and Romsey and in 1771 Parliament was petitioned for leave to bring in a Bill. Unfortunately lack of support meant that the Bill failed. A revival occurred in 1788 and this time received the backing of the Corporation of Andover and a subscription of £35,000 was ordered. A Bill was presented to Parliament in

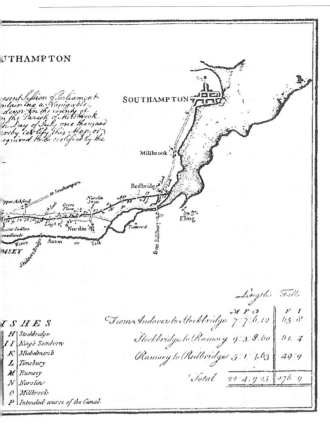

41. Seal of the Andover Canal Company 1789.

March 1789 and received the royal assent on 13 July. The Andover to Redbridge Canal was completed about May 1794; it was 22 miles long with a fall to sea level of 179ft by 24 locks to take craft 65ft x 8ft 6in. It was never a great success, but it served a local purpose, carrying agricultural produce from the Andover district and bringing coal and building materials up from Southampton Water to Romsey, Stockbridge and Andover.

In 1800 a poem appeared in the *Gentleman's Magazine* attributed to the Poet Laureate, Henry James Pye, about the Andover Canal:

"Southampton's wise sons found their river so large,
Tho' 'twould carry a Ship, 'twould not carry a barge,
But soon this defect their sage noddles suppl'd
For they cut a snug ditch to run close by its side.
Like the man who, contriving a hole through his wall
To admit his two cats, the one great, t'other small.
Where a great hole was made for great puss to pass through,
Had a little hole cut for his little cat too."

FRENCH PRISONERS

During the mid-18th century, when Britain was at war with France, a large number of refugees, French prisoners of war and officers on parole were in the town. Several of them married Andover girls and one such marriage was later to play a significant part in the French Revolution. Jean Drouett and Elizabeth Atkins were married in Andover church on 5 January, 1762, by the curate, John Stable.

A short while later, Jean and Elizabeth had a son, whom they christened Jean Baptiste. This same Jean Baptiste Drouett returned to France and became Postmaster of St Menhoulde, Marne, and it was his information that led to the arrest of the fugitive Louis XVI at Varennes (50 miles north of Paris) in July 1791. Drouett was well rewarded for his contribution to the Revolution and in 1792 he became a member of the French National Convention and was elected to the Council of Five Hundred in 1796.

ANDOVER LOYAL VOLUNTEERS

At this period of struggle with revolutionary France and the empire of Napoleon, Hampshire was put on alert of invasion and several local volunteer bodies were formed. The newspapers at this time were full of accounts of local standards being raised. The Andover Loyal Volunteers were established at this time and their standard can be seen on display in Andover Museum.

Often the French and Russian refugees and officers had temporary residence in Andover, living with residents as lodgers. The main area where they were quartered was around Sopers Lane (now West Street) and what is now covered by the Chantry Way town centre development. They also had their own improvised chapel in that locality. After 23 April 1814 the officers were no longer classed as prisoners of war and many remained in the town where they had met their wives or had built up business interests.

Refugees, including gentry and clergy, fleeing from the French Revolution, also arrived in Hampshire. The headmaster of Andover Grammar School, Revd William Peddar was also curate of the parish and befriended many of them. A letter of thanks to Peddar from the venerable Bishop of S. Pol de Leon, who was living with others at the King's House in Winchester is of interest:

> LONDON, 16 Sept 1802.
>
> Sir,   The promptitude with which you complied with my favour of the 14th inst. demands my sincere thanks, but I cannot sufficiently acknowledge the Sympathising Kindness and generous liberality expressed in every part of your most friendly Letter which I shall transmit together with the Certificate: convinced that the contents of the former will afford a consoling palliative of the latter, and the Friends of the Deceased will share with me the satisfaction that our Country-Man had merited the esteem of Persons so highly respectable of a Nation which claims our eternal gratitude.
>
>   I remain with the greatest consideration,
>
>   Sir,
>
>   Your truly obliged humble servant.
>   (signed) + j M en. DE LEON.

It was customary at that time for French prisoners of war in Andover to attend divine service on Sunday mornings, followed by 'convivial meetings' at Bowling Green House (latterly known as the Folly Inn). Those of the prisoners who stayed on in the town were later more politely referred to as the French 'visitors'. James Lock was landlord of Bowling Green House in 1790, and his daughter Elizabeth married Jean Martin Louis Coutier, one of the prisoners, on 24 October 1811 at Andover church.

Bowling Green House was named after the bowling green said to have been laid sometime around 1550. A Friendly Society was formed there in 1838 when the inn was known as the Antelope. Later called the Cut Hedge and then the Folly Inn, it was pulled down in 1969 and a new public house built a little to the left and to the rear of the old building.

Other French refugees are mentioned in the Andover burial records:

> 13 Sept., 1793, Francis Lirochons (aged 26), suicide
>
> 16 Aug., 1797, Louis Charles de Carne (about 25) buried in Mr John Nosworthy's tomb
>
> 3 Nov., 1813, Michael Marie Coie (aged 31)

It would seem that Francis Lirochons had a disappointment in love and committed suicide, but many other Frenchmen had more fruitful relationships as the marriage registers show:

> 29 May 1814, Hyacinths Francis de Villedon and Jane Rumsey
>
> 15 Jan. 1815, Charles Aubertin and Harriet Sedgley

The baptism registers are also interesting for the following:

> 17 July, 1811, John Adolph, son of Francis and Deborah Lepaire.
>
> 11 Dec., 1811, Marie Charlotte Louise Manoela Francisca de Poula, daughter of Louis and Francis Patch Geron.
>
> 7 Oct., 1812, Louise Henriette Rosalie, daughter of J.M.L. and E. Coutier.
>
> 11 March, 1814, Mary Ann, daughter of Andrew F. and Deb. Lapaire.
>
> 26 April.,1815. Louis Etienne. son of J.M.L. & E. Coutier.
>
> 13 Dec., 1815, Chas. Thos., son of Ch. and H. Aubertin.
>
> 10 July, 1822, William, son of CH. and H. Aubertin.

On 5 November 1811 a large fire was caused by a skyrocket falling onto a thatched barn in East

Street. Five houses and two barns containing hops, grain and livestock were destroyed. Some of the French officers on parole helped the fire fighters and were recommended to the Transport Board for favourable consideration.

A letter survives, reprinted in Bennett & Parson's *History of the Andover Grammar School:*

H.M.S. Guildford,
the 15th October, 1813.

To the Most Reverend Mr Peder at Andover.
RESPECTABLE SIR,

It is from a prison ship that I take the Liberty to trouble you (in your so precious occupations. to the inhabitants of the town which has the happiness to possess you) to beseech you to agree my sincere gratitudes, for all favours that your generous heart and your humanity have pleased themselves to Bestow on my Spouse and Child, as well as your most Worthy and respectable Consort, Without forgetting your kind and dear daughter and Son. Pray you, Sir, be so good as to Continue your Kindness towards an unhappy family, which apply to you with the confidence, you will not refuse this humble request to obtain from you a Certificate in duplicate, explaining (Truth and but Truth) it is to say that the 5th November, 1811 the fire break-out into the town of Andover, about 8 in the evening, and that Louis Giro, hospitals director, prisoner of War on parole has by a supernatural movement quitted his wife Who was in shild-bed, to fly to the assistance of the unhappy inhabitants and their property, and retired himself after the conflagration was entirely abated; though his presence was equally very urgent near his spouse; since it is certain that it was the 7th of the same month at 8 in the morning that she was delivered, that the certificate is from I first, to make my spouse and shild enjoy to the half pay, and second to join it to a petition tending to solicit the diminution of my hard captivity.

I believe, Sir, that it is necessary that this certificate may be signed by several persons, on that, I refer myself to your decision

Giron

Towards the end of September 1812, eight of the officers on parole escaped from the town on horseback, but they were recaptured about a fortnight later at Hordle, near Christchurch.

Yet another Andover woman, Harriet Sedgley, married a French ex-POW Charles Aubertin in January 1815. Though he wanted her to go back to France with him, she preferred to stay and all was well until after the birth of their first child that year. Again Aubertin attempted to persuade her to go to France with him but again she refused. Eventually he returned home alone in 1817. He kept up correspondence and sent money back to help her and about 1820 came back to Andover to again induce her to go with him. Harriet would not and after the birth of their second son in 1822 he waited no longer and returned to France. He was never heard from again. By this time Harriet decided she had to find employment to look after her children and had set up a loom for silk weaving at her house in London Terrace, Vigo Lane (Vigo Road), where she died in 1829 at the age of 31. Descendants of the Aubertin family are still resident in the village of Amport, near Andover.

BREWING, BANKING AND COAL

No history of Andover in the 18th and 19th centuries would be complete without mention of the Heath family, for they worked their way into almost every aspect of local life during that time. The family originated in Warwickshire and can date its lineage back to 1580 when Ralph Heath became keeper of deer to the Duke of Bolton, who owned estates at Hackwood Park, Basingstoke. He later went on to become Ranger of Alice Holt Forest. His son Edmund, a farmer, lived at Headley and was a convert of George Fox, through which association he joined the Society of Friends.

It was Ralph's great grandson Charles (1740-1810), who came to Andover from Alton about 1770 and purchased a large Queen Anne property in London Street, the site of a former inn. For many years known as Savoy Chambers, the building has today gone back to its roots as a 'Hogshead' public house. To start a brewing business must have seemed anathema to the Quaker community, but that was what Charles did and a very successful business it became too. He built the brewery next door in the area now occupied by the DHSS and HM Inspector of Taxes building.

He also developed another aspect when he went into partnership with a man called Stratton and together founded a wine and spirit business. Over the years Charles gradually brought his three sons into the business, Charles Jnr., Thomas and William Hawkins, and on his death the business

42. Thomas Heath (1781-1842), son of Charles Heath, founder of Andover Bank in London Street. Thomas had a liking for sundials and had one placed on the bank and on Heath House. He was mayor of Andover in 1837.

43. The offices of Your Move, estate agents, formerly the site of Heath's Bank 1790-1847 (photograph 2001).

passed to a co-partnership of the three. Charles Jnr. was responsible for making a huge profit for the business when he obtained a contract to supply beer to a large militia camp stationed at Winchester in anticipation of a French invasion.

Charles senior had, in 1791, set up another partnership with Thomas Gilbert, a man who one year earlier had founded an Andover bank under the name Gilbert and Co. It traded under this name until 1809 when it was changed to Heath and Co. and the premises moved opposite Charles' home to no. 33 London Street, currently the offices of 'Your Move', estate agents. The bank building survives today, with the sundial over the door, a trademark of the Heath family. William Hawkins Heath built his home next door to Savoy Chambers and called it Heath House, placing a sundial in the wall. This building survived until 1936, when it was pulled down to make way for the Savoy cinema and as a mark of respect the sundial was incorporated into the back wall of the cinema.

According to a catalogue of British provincial banknotes the bank issued two £5 notes, one in the name of Gilbert and Co. and the other in the

name of Heath and Co., although neither of these appear to have survived. Heath's Bank was incorporated into the Hampshire Banking Company in 1861, which itself went through a series of takeovers before being amalgamated with Lloyds Bank in 1918.

An accounts book survives covering the years 1783 to 1810, listing the various properties, inns, alehouses etc. owned by the family in an area stretching from Highclere in the north of the county to Winchester, fifteen miles south of Andover. Over twenty hostelries were served by the brewery amongst which were the Three Choughs, the Lower Angel (now the Foresters) and the Coopers Arms. The book also lists payments made for shares during the promotional phase of the Andover–Redbridge Canal and by 1798 it would seem the family owned "Eight Shares in the River" at a total cost of £800.

The Heaths used the Andover Canal to bring coal to the town. Also of note in the book is the 'Booth on Weyhill', alluding to a beer tent or similar. The Heath Brewery business was offered for sale in 1847 together with lands and the bank. Savoy Chambers was sold to Frederick Ellen, together with the bank building, the booth on Weyhill, and other lands acquired as a direct

44. *Andover Theatre c.1803. "It stood in a dirty lane leading from the upper end of Andover to Newbury." (See p60)*

result of the 1812 Enclosure Act.

Charles Heath senior died in 1810 and was buried in Alton. His two sons William Hawkins and Thomas were active in local politics and both became mayors of Andover, William in 1834-35, 1840-41 and 1851-52 and Thomas in 1837-38. Thomas whilst in office laid the foundation stone for Andover Gasworks in June 1838.

"THE NOISIEST GALLERY IN THE KINGDOM"

In 1803, the Andover Theatre was opened in Newbury Street by a man named Thornton, who owned other theatres at Fareham and Gosport. Priory Lodge presently stands on the site of the building. Thornton's associate in the venture was Thomas Rawlins, a printer, who built the theatre at his own expense. In the *Theatre Tourist*, published in 1805, the theatre is described: "it stands in a dirty lane, leading from the upper end of Andover to Newbury, is on a small scale, but being new has a clean appearance". By 1842 it had been demolished, having gained the reputation during its short life as being "the noisiest gallery in the kingdom".

Before the Andover Theatre, most theatrical performances had taken place in a large thatched barn at the rear of the Angel Inn which Thornton had leased from around 1787 until 1800 when the barn was sold to the Society of Friends or Quakers. According to the *Theatre Tourist* another impresario, a Mr Bowles, put on plays in a large malthouse or barn around the year 1770, but never appeared more than once in two or three years.

DRAPERS AND BANKERS

The Wakeford family, which went on to become well known in the Andover district as bankers and woollen drapers, first appears in 1717 when Joseph Wakeford of Odiham married Mary Brice of Andover. Both families were non-conformists. Joseph continued trading in Odiham, with his half-brother William, until about 1744 when he moved his family and share of the business to Andover, after buying his brother-in-law's interest in a shop and house in the High Street for about £590. He traded as a mercer and woollen draper and was elected to the town's Company of Haberdashers in 1744, serving as its Master Warden for 1745-6. Joseph Wakeford jnr was brought into the business in 1745 and they ran it together until Joseph senior's death ten years

later. They also traded as ironmongers having bought up the stock of his wife's Uncle Brice when he purchased the shop. The ironmongery trade continued until 1771 when that part of the business was sold to a local man, Samuel Fennell, for £715 12s 8d.

The Wakefords were probably acting as bankers way in advance of the official start of the earliest surviving cashbook which dates from 1759, for interspersed in the company's day books are references to drafts and bills. Joseph jnr had two sons by his second marriage, William Steele and Samuel, who were to take a large part in the Wakeford Bank. It was the practice of the country banks to employ an agent to handle their transactions with the London money markets. In 1759 such business of the Wakeford bank was handled by Messrs Brassey, Lee and Son and, as the business expanded, by Messrs Ayton, Brassey, Lee & Salterthwaite of 71 London Street. The Lees were great friends and business associates of the Wakefords and a daughter of both Joseph and Brice (his younger brother) both married a member of the Lee family. Joseph jnr died in 1785 leaving a small estate in Enham to his daughter, Mary and virtually everything else to his son and partner William Steele Wakeford.

William Steele was now running the business, which still traded as woollen drapers and bankers. He was very active in the promotion of the Andover Canal and became treasurer when the Act was finally passed. The late 1790s was a difficult time for the banking business countrywide. A general crisis in confidence, a direct result of the Revolution in France, made businessmen nervous and they began to withdraw money from banks in large amounts, straining the resources of the Bank of England and putting many of the country banks into liquidation. As a result there was a severe shortage of currency in circulation and local banks, including Wakeford's and Heath's, issued their own banknotes and token coinage. Wakeford's notes, emblazoned 'Andover Old Bank' were issued in £10, £5 and £1 denominations and many survive to this day in museums and private collections. The Wakeford tokens, like their notes, carry the town crest and state on one side 'Andover Token' and on the reverse 'Payable by W.S & I Wakeford'; they are to the value of either one shilling or one penny. In all twelve different types and denominations of coin were manufactured by Thomas Halliday, die-maker, of Newhall Street, Birmingham. An Act of Parliament removed the silver

45. *The Andover Borough Scale Beam and Standard Yard dated 1826.*

46. *The Andover Borough standard weights and measures, which were used to decide arguments and disputes at all fairs and markets in and around the town.*

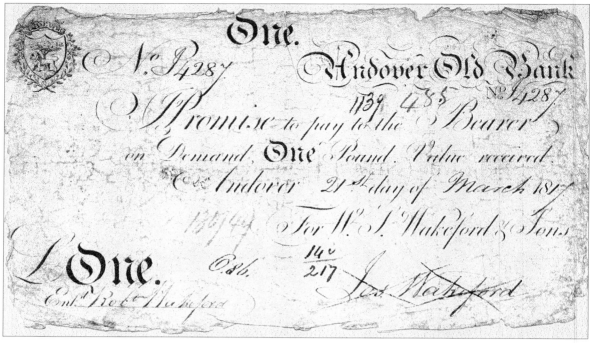

47. A one pound note dated March 1817, issued by Wakeford's Andover Old Bank.

tokens from circulation in 1813, but the copper coins were allowed to continue until 1817.

The Wakeford banking business showed signs of financial stress by around 1815 and the family estate at East Tytherley was rented out to help defray mounting debts. In 1819 they borrowed money from Lee and Co. and this was the start of a serious decline. The estate had to be sold, and they had to accept an offer of £69,000 for East Tytherley Manor House. The government was insisting that the country banks cease the issuing of further banknotes and this put greater stress on an already bad situation. By 1825 all the country banks found themselves in a panic as people began to withdraw their money. Andover Old Bank only just managed to survive this, but by February 1826 Lee and Co. had seen enough. The Wakefords were ordered to put their house in order or their overdraft would be withdrawn and they later refused to pay out on promissory notes to Heath's Bank. On Saturday 4 March 1826 the doors of Wakeford's Bank closed and the company was later declared bankrupt.

In the Dorset Record Office is a collection of documents of the Rev. Thomas Racket and his family (17th to 19th century) and in bundle 78 there is a letter from a Mrs Blunt to Mrs Racket (undated but *c*.1830):

> I think it right to tell you not to trust money in Country Banks – the Cash we have had in the failure of Wakeford's at Andover has been a 2nd deluge in the Country all around: - the number whom it has involved are past counting.

In the electoral roll of 1833 a Joseph Wakeford is described as being resident at Cricklade. However, this must have been the last year of his residence there for the manor of Cricklade was sold in two lots in January 1833 and May 1833 to help pay for the dividends paid to the bank's creditors. He is mentioned as a Freeman of the Borough, entitled to vote in the election of a Member or Members for the Borough of Andover and was burgess of the Corporation in 1830.

After the business failed all three brothers left the district. Joseph and his wife moved to Devon, whilst William and Robert moved to Southampton and by 1834 were trading together again as wine and spirit merchants, where they remained in business for a further 30 years.

The Iron Man of Andover

LORD NELSON IN ANDOVER

In 1800 Lord Nelson and Lady Hamilton were in Andover and spent the night at the Star and Garter Hotel (now the Danebury Hotel) en route to Salisbury to receive the Freedom of the City. He was a friend of Capt. Henry Festing, RN and the story is told how Admiral Lord Nelson in 1805 was entertained to tea in Festing's house, which is now Andover Museum, whilst on his last journey seawards to embark at Southampton. The Rev. John Greenly, who became schoolmaster at Andover Grammar School from 1810-1812 had been a chaplain to Nelson on the *Revenge* and was present at Trafalgar on 21 November 1805 where he, Greenly, was wounded and in consequence received a pension.

Oddly, the cloak in which Nelson was wrapped after being critically wounded at Trafalgar came to reside in the old Andover Museum. How it came to be is a mystery. The ticket attached to it bore the words 'Cloak in which Lord Nelson was wrapped when wounded on the 21st of October 1805. This cloak was given to the late Admiral Rawlins Thompson by the late Sir Thomas Hardy.' It has since been transferred to the National Maritime Museum at Greenwich.

THE IRON MAN OF ANDOVER

The story of the founding of Tasker's of Andover begins in 1781 in Wiltshire when Stephen Tasker, a village blacksmith, married Ann Goodwing. Over a period of 21 years Ann produced no less than ten children. There were seven sons, the oldest of which was Robert (born 1785) and he became apprenticed to his father in the blacksmith's shop. By 1806 Robert considered he was proficient enough to earn his own living as a journeyman blacksmith. One of the reasons for his leaving home was his faith – he was a staunch nonconformist, but his father was not a believer.

Reaching the Andover/Weyhill area Robert heard that the blacksmith at Abbotts Ann needed an assistant, and a man named Maslen took him on. He worked for him for three years. He was a thrifty and religious man and through self-denial and without a family to support he purchased a small house and garden near the blacksmith's shop. In 1809 he took over the business from Maslen. Doing well, he returned home to Wiltshire to claim his childhood sweetheart, Martha Fowle, and they married and returned to Abbotts Ann. Each Sunday he travelled into

48. Lord Nelson.

49. Robert and Mary Tasker at work in the forge at Abbotts Inn. (From 'The Poor Blacksmith made Rich', by Rev. Richard Knill, c.1840.)

50 & 51. Two engines produced by Tasker. Above is his first 12hp self-moving or 'traction' engine built c.1871, front steering. Below is the 'Economic' type traction engine, introduced in 1891.

52. *Waterloo Iron Works, Anna Valley near Andover, c.1895.*

Andover to attend the Independent or Congregational chapel, now the United Reform Church in East Street. Religious differences were common and occasionally provoked violence. On one occasion he was holding a religious meeting in his house when a group of armed men broke in and beat up some of the party.

It was not the only occasion that his religion had caused him difficulty and an attack on his life was made on a return trip from Andover, but he confronted his would-be assailant who fled into the shadows. Work was short and he travelled further and further to sell his skills. Robert's credibility returned after he invented a design for a plough, ideally suited for the chalk uplands of Hampshire, and business improved greatly. He needed a partner and persuaded his younger brother William to join him. They soon outgrew the blacksmith's shop and found an ideal site for a new one at Anna Valley, where they harnessed water power. In 1813 they opened a foundry and works, getting ever larger, but during the riots of labourers in 1830 the Waterloo Iron Works, as it was known, was attacked and partially wrecked by a mob from Andover.

Robert retired in 1836 leaving the business to his brother, but not before purchasing a new house in Upper Clatford and a property in Andover High Street, both called Waterloo House, as an investment. William shortly afterward took

on as a partner George Fowle. A speciality of the company was cast iron bridges of which there are many dotted all over the county. They branched out into farm machinery design and the manufacture of well-boring machines, wagons and carts. They also became selling agents for other manufacturers' machines. From farm implements the firm switched to making steam engines in 1865, and later, trailers, in which the present company specialised until it closed in 1980.

Tasker's was the first industrial concern to develop in the Andover area, and the first of its big employers. Gradually they were followed by other industries of an agricultural flavour – Watson and Haig, Pitt's, McDougall's and Hovis the millers, all catering principally for the needs of the farming community.

MURDER OF A GAMEKEEPER
On 17 December 1821, the headline of the *Salisbury and Wiltshire Journal* proclaimed 'Barbarous Murder Committed by Poachers'. It was reporting on the inquest at Tidworth, near Andover, on the body of Robert Baker, the gamekeeper of Thomas Ashetton Smith of Tidworth House. It went on to tell how it was the usual practice for Mr Ashetton Smith's gamekeepers to keep a lookout for poachers after dark and that seven had assembled at midnight on 6 December in

Ashdown Coppice for that purpose. They were in the wood for about an hour when the sound of a shot was heard. The gamekeepers proceeded to the area where the shot had been heard and three men were discovered.

The poachers threatened to shoot the first man who tried to apprehend them; Baker called their bluff and went forward to arrest them, whereupon the youngest poacher snatched the gun his partner was holding, pointed it at Baker's chest and fired, killing him instantly. In the fight that followed, the poachers badly beat up the remaining gamekeepers, stole one of their guns, but left behind their own weapons and their hats. The newspaper described the whole incident as 'characteristic of the amateurish'.

The coroner's jury returned a verdict of wilful murder and on 16 March 1822 the newspaper reported that two of the poachers had been apprehended by Bow Street police officers and were then lodged in Andover Gaol. The prisoners, according to the *Journal*, had "impeached their accomplices for which a strict search is being made". The two men detained in Andover Gaol were a young labourer named as James Turner,

53. Thomas Ashetton Smith. He was MP for Andover 1821-31 and probably the most famous huntsman England has ever known. He lived at Tidworth House, Tidworth.

and Edmund Steele and, no doubt under mixed threats and blandishments, they told the whole story of that night's incidents and of the four mile trek back to Andover from Ashdown Coppice.

Thomas Ashetton Smith was MP for Andover from May 1821 until 1831, after succeeding his father to the position. 'Tom Smith', as his father always called him, was a fanatical huntsman and his interest in politics came a poor second. He put up a reward of one hundred pounds for information that would lead to the arrest of Robert Goodall, James Goodall and James Scullard, all described as labourers of Andover. Despite the Bow Street Runners' hot pursuit and a detailed description of the missing men they were not caught, and in addition the keepers were unable to swear with certainty who had fired the fatal shot. The authorities appear to have decided that Turner was the one to take the blame for the crime and encouraged the other prisoner, Steele, to turn king's evidence. Local opinion placed some doubt over Turner's guilt and the *Journal*, not known for any radical views, said that "the case of this unfortunate man has excited uncommon commiseration in the public mind", adding that his family were well respected in Andover.

Turner lived in Brick-kiln Street, now known as Winchester Street, where the family trade was bricklaying and more than likely brick makers too. The family held the licence of the Three Tuns Inn at the junction of East Street and London Street. The Goodalls were a noted New Street family and a William Goodall was licensee of the Pelican Inn in 1825.

James Turner was sent to Winchester Gaol to await trial at the Spring Assizes in 1822. He was tried alongside a Romsey poacher, Charles Smith, accused of shooting at one of Lord Palmerston's gamekeepers. Both men were found guilty and were hanged for their crimes.

THE HEAVYWEIGHT CHAMPIONSHIP OF GREAT BRITAIN

A barefist fight billed as 'The Heavyweight Championship of Great Britain' took place on Finkley Down, just off the Smannell Road outside the town on 20 May 1823. The title had remained dormant since 1812, when Tom Cribb had retired, and two contenders, Thomas Spring from Hereford and Will Neat from Bristol, were nominated to fight. It was one of the biggest events Andover had ever staged and thousands were drawn to the area. All the inns and taverns were full and those who could not find an inn were obliged to

54. *Tom Spring, featured on a Staffordshire plaque, c.1825.*

put up with any shelter they could find. The sports journal of its day, the *Sporting Intelligence,* complained that the Andover innkeepers had put up their prices to match the occasion.

The fans were infuriated when local magistrates called upon the mayor and his colleagues to stop the fight being held. The mayor, afraid of a riot, allowed it to proceed. It was estimated that over 30,000 men *and* women attended.

When the fighters eventually appeared Thomas Spring had Tom Cribb as his second, and in William Neat's corner was another well-known fighter of his day, Tom Belcher. The boxers fought for a purse of £200 but many thousands of pounds had been staked on them. At the outset the two looked evenly matched, but by the sixth round Spring was on top having knocked Neat to the ground on several occasions. In the eighth round Neat was forced to retire through an injured arm.

It was a great disappointment to many who had bet heavily on Neat and a number of fights broke out around the ring. Neat was accused of selling the fight and he flatly refuted the allegations, saying, "he had done his best".

An enquiry was set up to discuss the allegations against Neat and an Andover surgeon, Richard R. Perry, confirmed that Neat's injuries were genuine and wrote a letter to that effect to the leading boxing official at the fight. This seems to have done the trick, for Neat was cleared of the charges and all the bets were paid out in full.

A PRINTING PIONEER

In 1823 John Benjamin Bensley set up a printing business in Sopers Lane (now West Street) in premises that had previously been occupied by Joseph Wakeford of Wakeford's Bank. His brother Thomas acted as principal proof-reader and lived in a newly erected house in Winchester Street.

The Bensleys' father, Thomas senior, had also been in printing. With Fredrich Konig, a German who came to England in 1806, he helped to construct a steam-powered printing press and together they developed a platen press capable of 400 impressions an hour, later going on to produce a steam-powered cylinder machine that could print 800 sheets an hour. Two of these presses were ordered for *The Times* and the first edition of the paper produced on the new press appeared on 29 November 1814. The joint efforts of both Bensley and Konig were described as "the greatest improvement connected with printing since the discovery of the art itself."

Thomas Bensley senior (d. 1833) began his own printing business in 1814 in London's Fleet Street. His offices in Bolt Court had been previously occupied by Edward Allen, the friend of Dr Johnson. In 1819 and again about 1822, fire destroyed Bensley's premises, together with much of its valuable stock. Soon after the last fire he moved to Andover to join his son John. John Bensley, working in close co-operation with his father, transferred many books from Bolt Court to Andover, including several written by William Cobbett – his *Rural Rides* was first published in 1830 – and many other of Cobbett's books were printed in Andover, including *A Grammar of the English Language* and *Advice to Young Men.*

The Andover factory was threatened during the Agricultural Riots of 1830. John Bensley narrowly avoided having his newly installed machinery wrecked by giving the rioters beer money, after which the men determined to concentrate on Tasker's foundry.

A period of national and trade depression followed these riots and it was not long before the Bensley business was sold out to Joseph Billing and, in order to be nearer to London, the plant was moved to Woking.

THE SILKWEAVERS

Andover's wool weaving industry had by the nineteenth century gone into steep decline, but according to Pigot's Directory of 1823 silkweaving was beginning to emerge as a new industry. This may have happened as a direct result of the large number of French prisoners of war quartered in the town after the Napoleonic War, but the two silk manufacturers mentioned in the directory were George Ransom and Thomas Tarrant. By 1851 the industry was in the hands of one man, James Pain. He owned a mill in London Road where he employed around 90 people, mostly women, manufacturing silks and velvets. According to the census that year, all the weaving was done on hand looms in the factory and there were only about a half dozen women employed as silk winders to supply the factory with pirns (bobbins). Some of the younger girls were labourers, sweeping around the looms etc.

Eastfield House now occupies the site of the mill, then described as being in 'Mud Town'. Eastfield Cottages on the east side of Eastfield Road are all that are left of a long row of silkweavers' cottages built nearby. James Pain himself lived in one of them with his wife, three children, his brother aged 14 and a 12-year-old

56. No. 45 Vigo Road, once the Silkweavers' Arms, the only pub the road had although it was one of the longest and most heavily populated roads in the town. Its licence ceased around 1850 when the building became a private house. It was demolished in 1978 to make way for new development.

house servant. There were many rows of silkweavers' cottages all over the town. Vigo Road, then known as London Lane, had its share and could also boast its own alehouse, the Silkweavers' Arms. Marlborough Street, East Street, Chantry Street are only a few of the areas of silkweavers' cottages mentioned in the 1851 census.

55. Former silkweavers' houses in Eastfield Road, in the area once known as 'Mud Town'. Photograph taken 1977.

57. Vigo Road c.1910. Note the silkweavers' cottages (London Row) in the background.

It was a time of great unemployment and poverty and we find that a high percentage of the women working at the factory had husbands out of work. A large number of the men were described as "Paupers, formerly Agricultural Workers".

The Andover Silk Mill did not have a very long life, for it is described in White's Directory of 1856 as "attracting much attention on its bankruptcy."

THE GEORGE INN

The George Inn in the High Street was a popular resort in the nineteenth century. It was "kept by one Sutton, a rich old fellow, who wore a round-skirted sleeved fustian waistcoat, with a dirty white apron tied around his middle and with no coat on." In the summer of 1826 local landowners were meeting in a 'snug' there, among them Sir John Pollen of Redenham, Bethel Cox of Quarley, Lascelles Iremonger of Wherwell and Henry Marsh, MP for Salisbury. They were intending to pass a resolution in favour of the corn laws but were thwarted by the sudden appearance of Henry Hunt, the 'Orator', who overturned their argument, leaving them in defeat and confusion.

William Cobbett spent many an enjoyable Saturday evening at the George, dining and talking into the early hours of the morning, at first resisted and later encouraged by landlord Sutton.

THE YEOMANRY CAVALRY

The Andover Yeomanry Cavalry was formed in 1832 as a result of the recent riots of agricultural workers. The Cavalry's first captain was Thomas Ashetton Smith of Tidworth House and his second in command and lieutenant was Ralph Etwall. Mr Sutton, a well-known local businessman, was the troop's cornet and carried the colours or pennant.

58. The George Inn, 1906, drawing by A.B. Connor.

The men used to train at the racing gallops at Weyhill and were reviewed on more than one occasion by the Duke of Wellington, who was a personal friend of Ashetton Smith. The only time the troop saw action was when it was mobilised to take part in the so called 'Battle of Kingsclere' to confront a large body of railway navvies that had gone on the rampage in the area. Rumour has it that when the rioters heard the Andover Cavalry were coming they fled in disorder, leaving the troopers with a bloodless victory.

Illustration 59 shows the Andover Cavalry on parade in the High Street, being reviewed by Ashetton Smith; they were disbanded in 1854.

59. Andover High Street, looking north toward the new Guild Hall in 1834. Capt. Ashetton Smith inspects the newly raised troop of Yeomanry Cavalry.

POWER TO THE PEOPLE

The Andover Lighting and Power Company was formed in June 1838 and lost no time in the erection of offices and a gas works, with the mayor laying the foundation stone on 5 July that year and lighting the first gas lamp in front of the Guildhall on 15 October. Described as a 'loyal' device, the lamp was in the shape of a star and the initial letters VR. The shareholders of the company dined at the George Inn to celebrate the event and the contractors were congratulated on the speedy completion of the work.

Toward the end of the century the company introduced the pre-payment meter, allowing the person of 'smaller means' to purchase gas at terms he could afford. By 1900 it became necessary to enlarge the gasworks and a new gasholder was on line by 1902. In 1926 demand was outstripping capacity and a virtual rebuilding of the works was necessary. In the winter of 1934/5 it was obvious that the 1902 gasholder was inadequate and a new holder was brought into use in September 1935.

Before gas lamps, oil lamps in the High Street were suspended on trees, and there was an oil lamp on the Town Bridge and another in Union Street.

THE FIRST POLICE FORCE

On 17 December 1839 Andover Borough Council voted to appoint two town's constables, ignoring the county force, which came into being at around the same time. By 1845 Andover had a head constable, three ordinary constables and a gaoler. but by 1846 the local force had amalgamated with the county force.

MAILCOACH HEYDAY

One of the fastest mailcoach services in the country passed through Andover on its way from London to the West Country. Known as the Devonport *Quicksilver*, the service started in 1826 in the heyday of the mailcoach era. Its journey began at the General Post Office in St Martin le Grand in London and the route took in Hounslow, Staines, Bagshot, Basingstoke, Andover, Amesbury, Wincanton, Ilchester, Ilminster, Honiton, Exeter, Chudleigh and Plymouth.

A time bill survives for the year 1837 which shows that the *Quicksilver* arrived in Andover at 2.20am. There was a 39-minute stopover, when the horses were changed for the next stage of the journey. A man named Broad had the contract for the changeover. In the book *Quicksilver*, by

60. The Weyhill Cheese Fair c.1860. The steward of the fair was Frederick Talbot (fifth from right), the tall man in a top hat. A policeman from the local force guards the truckles of cheese.

TIME-BILL, LONDON, EXETER AND DEVONPORT ("QUICKSILVER") MAIL, 1837.

Contractors' Names.	Number of Passengers (In. / Out.)	Stages (M. F.)	Time Allowed (H. M.)	Despatched from the General Post Office, the of , 1837, at 8 p.m.
				Coach No. {With timepiece sent out safe, No. to
				Arrived at the Gloucester Coffee-House at .
Chaplin		12 2		Hounslow.
		7 1		Staines.
		9 7	2 47	Bagshot. Arrived 10.47 p.m.
		9 1		Hartford Bridge.
Company		10 1		Basingstoke.
		8 0	2 54	Overton.
		3 5		Whitchurch. Arrived 1.41 a.m.
Broad		6 7	0 39	Andover. Arrived 2.20 a.m.
Ward		13 7	1 19	Amesbury. Arrived 3.39 a.m.
Davis		9 5	0 55	Deptford Inn. Arrived 4.34 a.m.
		0 5		Wiley.
		6 5	0 41	Chicklade. Arrived 5.15 a.m. (Bags dropped for Hindon, 1 mile distant.)
		6 6		Mere.
		7 0		Wincanton.
Whitmash		13 4	2 59	Ilchester.
		4 1		Cart Gate. Arrived 8.14 a.m.
		2 6		Water Gore, 6 miles from South Petherton.
Jeffery			0 44	Bags dropped for that place.
		5 1		Ilminster. Arrived 8.58 a.m. Dep. 9.23.
Soaring		8 1	0 25 / 0 46	Yarcombe, Heathfield Arms. Arrived 10.9 a.m.
		8 7	0 51	Honiton. Arrived 11 a.m.
Wheaton		16 4	1 34	Exeter. Arrived 12.34 p.m.
			0 10	Ten minutes allowed.
Cockram		10 3		Chudleigh.
		9 3	1 57	Ashburton. Arrived 2.41 p.m.
		13 2		Ivybridge.
		6 6		Bags dropped at Ridgway for Plympton, 3 furlongs distant.
Elliott		4 0	2 33	Plymouth. Arrived at the Post Office, Devonport, the of , 1837, at 5.14 p.m. by timepiece. At by clock.
		1 7		Coach No. {Delivered timepiece safe, No. to . arr.
		216 1	21 14	

The time of working each stage is to be reckoned from the coach's arrival,

61. Time table for the London-Exeter-Devonport 'Quicksilver' Royal Mail, 1837.

R. C. & J. M. Anderson, there is mention of one coachman, 24-year-old Harry Ward, who drove the coach from Andover to Salisbury and who, it says, was proud of the fact he had never had an accident on any road. Harry is reputed to have replied in answer to a question by a passenger, 'This is the twentieth brandy and water today but you soon get it blown out of you crossing Salisbury Plain'.

In an incident just outside Andover at Abbotts Ann, a shaft of a wagon broke during the descent of Abbots Hill and ran into the off-wheeler horse of the *Quicksilver* mail, killing it outright. The coachman, named Simpson, and the guard were thrown right over the horses' heads, landing on the dead wheeler. They continued their journey after re-harnessing the horses' pickaxe style, with one leader and drove to the next change at the Winterslow Hut (Pheasant Inn).

THE EXETER MAIL ATTACKED BY LION

On 20 October 1816, the same Pheasant Inn was the scene of one of the most famous of the coaching dramas. The coachman of the Exeter up-mail, when approaching the inn, noticed what he thought was a young calf trotting alongside the coach. As he stopped to drop off the letter-bag, a large lioness, which had escaped from a travelling menagerie, pounced upon the offside leader horse. The terrified passengers fled from the coach and bolted themselves in the inn, leaving the coachman and guard to cope with the situation.

The guard, Joseph Pike, drew his blunderbuss and was about to fire at the animal, when the menagerie owner, who had tracked it to Winterslow, and who didn't want to lose such a valuable asset, stopped him. The real hero of the day was a large mastiff dog, belonging to the landlady of the inn, which rushed out and attacked the lioness. The dog survived a mauling and escaped and hid under a granary at the back of the inn. The inn's ostlers managed to calm the horses that were panicking, and eventually the lioness was captured.

The horse attacked was an ex-racehorse named Pomegranate, once the property of the Earl of Scarborough. It had been difficult on the racecourse and had been sent for steady work in the coaches, a not uncommon cure for excitable horses. The incident was a great sensation in the newspapers of the time, and a print by the well-known sporting and mailcoach artist, James Pollard, *(illustration 62)* featuring the incident, sold well. The horse was rested but later was back in harness and for years worked the Exeter Mail.

BUSY TIMES

The *Hampshire Directory* published by Pigot in 1840 shows that the White Hart in Bridge Street was the busiest hostelry in the town during the latter period of the coaching era. In addition to the *Quicksilver*, at least five other coaches used the inn including the Royal Mail from Exeter to London, which stopped at 11pm every night and 4am on the return journey. Originally the Royal Mail coach left from the Star and Garter Hotel but by 1840 the contract had been transferred to the White Hart.

Another coach from Exeter was the *Defiance*, which arrived at the White Hart at 6am and at midnight on the return journey. The *Magnet* from Weymouth called at 1pm each day on the trip to London and again at the same time on the return

62. *The Exeter Mail attacked. A lioness savaging the offside leader horse of the Exeter Mail at the Pheasant Inn (Winterslow Hut), 1816. Painting by James Pollard.*

63. The Andover Postboy. A carved and painted wooden model of a postboy c.1800, believed to be used as a trade-sign at the post office in the Star and Garter Inn, High Street. In his hand is a letter with Mr Marcer's name on it – he was the postmaster at the time.

journey, which took it on to Salisbury, Blandford, Dorchester, Bridport, Axminster and Honiton. The *New Salisbury* called in at 10am each day and at 3pm on its return and the *Hero* from Bridgewater arrived every Tuesday, Thursday and Saturday night at 10pm. Finally the *Plough*, which ran between Southampton and Cheltenham, called at the inn every Tuesday, Thursday and Saturday morning at eleven, travelling on to Marlborough, Swindon, Cricklade and Cirencester.

The other inns were not left out. The *Salisbury Flying Machine* called at the George in the High Street, and the *North Devon* from Barnstaple called at the Katherine Wheel in Bridge Street 'opposite the White Hart' every morning from Monday to Saturday. The *Phoenix* from Exeter and the *Traveller* also used the Katherine Wheel. Another from Devonport called the *Subscription* stopped at the Star and Garter, at the bottom of the High Street.

64. The Star and Garter Inn c.1900. One of the town's premier coaching inns and used as a post office in the late 18th and early 19th century.

65. The White Hart Hotel, Bridge Street, where the 'Defiance' from Exeter and the 'Magnet' from Weymouth stopped. (Photograph 1990).

THE ANDOVER TEMPERANCE SOCIETY

The *Hampshire Chronicle* reported on an event in Andover on Monday 8 June 1840:

On Monday, this town presented a most animating appearance in consequence of the celebration of their annual festival of teetotalers. Members of the Andover Auxiliary Temperance Society walked in procession through the crowded streets to the Town Hall, preceded by a band of music and banners. The members and friends of tee-totalism, to the number of 400, drank tea together in the Hall, after which a public meeting was held. The report stated the number of members to be 298, including 18 reclaimed drunkards.

CANAL CLOSURE

William Steele Wakeford, the Andover banker, was one of the promoters of the Andover Canal. In 1833 he transferred one of his shares to William Tasker, who in turn transferred it the following year to his younger brother William. Iron for the Tasker foundry came from South Wales, via Southampton and the Andover Canal, or from the Forest of Dean. The iron was then brought up via the Kennet and Avon Canal to Burbage and by road wagon to Andover. A waybill of the year the canal was closed shows that it took two days to transport six tons of iron from Redbridge to Tasker's wharf at Clatford.

Trade on the Andover-Redbridge Canal was not large enough to earn a dividend throughout its life, but had begun to pick up by 1851 when it was reported to be only one year behind with its loan interest. This was unfortunate, as this was the period when railway competition began.

Many attempts had been made over the years by railway companies to buy the canal so as to construct a railway along its route. In 1857 the Great Western Railway proposed to form the Andover to Redbridge Railway Company and in 1859 the canal ceased operations and was subsequently filled in. The railway line itself fell victim to the reforms advocated by Lord Beeching in 1964, but has more recently been turned into a delightful long-distance walk – the Test Way.

A GREAT BENEFACTOR

In 1809 the Revd William Stanley Goddard DD resigned the headmastership of Winchester College and came to live at Andover in a house which in 1845 he bequeathed to become the parish vicarage. The old vicarage in Newbury Street is

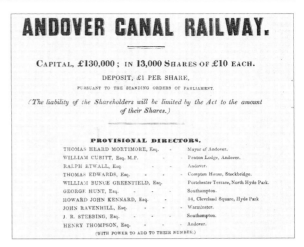

66. *Part of a prospectus for the Andover Canal Railway, 1859.*

today the office of solicitors. Goddard's wife, Henrietta Gale, was born in Andover and her niece Miss Martha Gale lived with them. The vicar at that time was the Revd Charles Henry Ridding, himself a Wykehamist but from a later generation. Dr Goddard took great interest in church matters and it was largely through his energies that the state of Foxcotte chapel was greatly improved from its almost ruinous condition. Another of his benefactions was the building in 1818 of the National School in his kitchen gardens in East Street, at a cost of almost £1,000.

Goddard then turned to the state of St Mary's church, which was too small for the greatly increasing population in the town and not imposing enough anyway. He engaged the services of a young architect, Augustus F. Livesey, to see if the seating accommodation could be increased by the erection of more galleries, but Livesey's reply was very non-committal and instead he recommended that all bellringing should cease as he considered the tower to be in a poor state.

It was not long before the word was out and exaggerated to state that the church was in a ruinous state. A meeting was held in 1840 "to consider the state of the church, a portion of which is considered by an eminent architect to be unsafe". Revd Ridding announced at that same meeting that "it was the unanimous opinion of the inhabitants that a new church should be erected." He further announced that plans had already been prepared for a new building, similar to that at Trowbridge in Wilts and which would be built free of charge to the parish.

67. The new parish church of St Mary, commissioned by Dr Goddard and opened for services on 11 August 1844.

REBUILDING THE CHURCH

Once again Mr Livesey was chosen as the architect, with Mr Dashwood of Ryde as the contractor, to demolish the Norman church and replace it with a new building. Work began in November 1840 with the arrival of stone from Normandy, being brought up by barge from Redbridge along the Andover Canal. By February 1841 the tower had disappeared but not as easily as had been expected, and explosives were used to aid the workmen. The vicar was having a bad time with the workmen on account of their "insolent bearing" and by autumn that year those that could not agree to curb their insolence were discharged.

Work continued slowly but by March 1842 the clerestory walls were finished and it was announced that the opening service could be held at Christmas that year. However on Friday 3 June at 5.30pm, just as the men had commenced work and most of them were on the roof, the north wall of the clerestory collapsed, the roof fell in and a number of the workmen fell 60 ft. William Bull was working below the wall and was killed. The following Monday evening the south clerestory wall also fell. Neither Dr Goddard nor the Revd Ridding were in Andover when the accident happened and so it was the duty of the curate, Mr Victor, to travel to London to break the news to Goddard.

Mr Livesey was insistent it was not his fault and indeed the inquest announced that the incident was an accident and that according to Mr Livesey there was some defect in no. 2 column. The real cause, as was found later, was that a Clerk of the Works had not been appointed and that there was insufficient strength of the clerestory walls. Despite this tragedy the work on the church continued and eventually the opening service was held on Sunday 11 August 1844, the tower being completed in January 1846.

Dr Goddard never saw this project to completion for he died on 10 October 1845 at the age of 88 at Brighton, where he was visiting "for the benefit of the sea-breezes".

The Workhouse Scandal

A ROYAL COMMISSION

The Labourers' Revolt or the Swing Riots led to a Royal Commission of Inquiry (1832) to study the reasons behind the rebellion of the poor. The age-old method of parish poor relief in place since Elizabeth I's day was now considered outdated and a system was needed in which the poor could be dealt with on a national level. The Inquiry recommended that the dole brought to the cottage or dwelling of the individual should be stopped and in its place relief would be provided only in workhouses at a huge reduction in expense, to be administered by a central commission.

The Inquiry suggested that workhouses would provide food and shelter and medical attention for the needy and the vagrants. It further recommended that those that did not wish to be included in the scheme could simply find some work and enjoy the benefits of freedom – this took no account of the general depression in farming over the last few years due to harsh winters and poor harvests.

The Royal Commission came under enormous criticism in the press, particularly in *The Times* with the owner, John Walter, commenting that he disliked the idea of a central commission poking its nose into local affairs; and most of all he abhorred the idea of workhouses. He considered it "a cruel experiment" to lock up people because they were poor and hungry and treating them like criminals, especially as the Commission had recommended impounding their remaining possessions.

THE NEW POOR LAW

Despite the outcry in the press and a tricky passage through both the Houses of Parliament, the Poor Law Reform Act of 1834 came into being. The Government's majority was huge and even the efforts of that arch critic of government, William Cobbett, fell on stony ground. The argument of Lord Althorp, in the Commons, and Lord Brougham in the Lords, was that "pauperism had to be removed or else, within the foreseeable future, the poor would increase to such an extent and the rates would rise to such a level that the country would suffer total bankruptcy."

There can be no argument that some action was necessary to improve the lot of the poor and get people back to work, but the Commissioners neglected to show proper justice or to treat the old, the children and the invalids with compassion. Often married couples were separated in the workhouses, children were removed from their parents and any communication between them was not allowed in communal areas.

Under the new Act, Hampshire was divided into 23 Unions. The Abingdon Union in Berkshire was the first in the country to be formed, on 1 January 1835, and by June that year the Andover Union was established.

Col. C.A. á Court, the assistant Poor Law Commissioner for Hampshire, Wiltshire and Dorset, arrived in Andover in a heat wave on 8 June 1835, and immediately set out to obtain the services of Henry Gawler, a local dignitary of Ramridge Cottage, Weyhill, Rev. Christopher Dodson of Penton Mewsey and Major Charles Gardiner.

THE ANDOVER UNION

At the Board of Guardians' first meeting in Andover Guildhall on 11 July 1835 the Rev. Dodson was appointed chairman with Hugh Stacpole of Clanville as his deputy; Thomas Lamb was appointed Clerk to the Union. The Union was divided into four districts as follows:

District No. 1
Andover, Foxcotte, Penton Mewsey, Penton Grafton, Appleshaw and Knights Enham
District No. 2
Tangley, Chute, Chute Forest, Hurstbourne Tarrant, Vernham's Dean, Linkenholt, Faccombe
District No. 3
Abbotts Ann, Longparish, Bullington, Barton Stacey, Wherwell, Goodworth Clatford, Upper Clatford, Chilbolton
District No. 4
Thruxton, Fyfield, Amport, Monxton, Quarley, Grateley, Shipton, Kimpton, Tidworth North, Tidworth South, Ludgershall

The Andover Union therefore served a population of almost 17,000. It was decided at the first meeting that a workhouse be built to house some 400 persons at or near Andover. The full committee at that meeting comprised of the following gentlemen: The Revd Christopher Dodson; the

68. Andover Workhouse, depicted in the Illustrated London News in 1846. The design was cruciform, creating four courtyards. The architect was Sampson Kempthorne.

Revd Henry B Green; Mr Northeast, Mr Noyes and Mr Baker.

In December 1835 Dodson wrote to Col. á Court to say that the Andover Board had decided that less accommodation was needed and that they planned to build a workhouse for 300 inmates in Bishops Court Lane (now Junction Road). The next letter to á Court in May 1836 described how differently the attitude of the labouring classes had changed, describing the opinion of the farmers that "…they have now a pleasure in employing men who apply civilly for work; and who when they are employed are anxious to please their masters." He went on to describe that work on the workhouse went on slowly, due to the difficulty in obtaining bricks, but he assured the Assistant Commissioner that by the winter they would be ready.

The architect of the workhouse was Sampson Kempthorne. It was based on a cruciform design that created four courtyards — one each for men, women, boys and girls. To the east of the site, the entrance block housed the Guardians' boardroom with receiving wards to either side.

While the Guardians waited for the building's completion, they set about organising the diet to be introduced, based on one of the standard diets proposed by the Poor Law Commissioners.

Unfortunately there was a mistake in their copy of the ingredients needed, which reduced the amounts of bread and vegetables to be given to the paupers. Near the end of 1836 they placed advertisements for the position of a Master of the Workhouse, at an annual salary of £80.

On Christmas Eve 1836, Sergeant-Major Colin McDougal was interviewed for the position. He was forty-four and retired from active service after a fall from a horse, which crushed his leg. He presented himself well and his wife also made an excellent impression. They appeared the ideal couple to the Guardians and so were offered employment. With McDougal's appointment Col. á Court's association with Andover ceased and a new Assistant Commissioner for Hampshire was appointed, William Henry Toovey Hawley, a hard man who enforced the letter of the law with heartless severity.

The Andover Union Workhouse opened its doors on 25 March 1837, when one hundred and eleven paupers became its first inmates. There should have been one more, Robert Gill, who had received the dole many times under the old system. He could not stand the thought of life inside the Workhouse walls and chose instead to take his own life. The Building Committee were very pleased with their work and described the

76. *A plaque on a house in Weyhill Road announcing the New Town scheme, founded by T. A. Banks in 1886. The plan was to populate outlying areas of Andover, but Weyhill, Millway, Plantation, St Hubert and Marchant Roads, and Newtown Close were the extent of the finished undertaking.*

the *Advertiser* for 110 years, until it was sold in 1986 to the Southern Newspapers Group. Over the years many changes have taken place – its format has changed from broadsheet to tabloid and a free *Andover Mid-Week Advertiser* introduced. The *Mid-Week* has recently been amalgamated with a rival free paper to become the *Avon Mid-Week Advertiser*. All printing now takes place in Basingstoke and the large offices at 10 High Street have given way to smaller premises in London Road.

HORSE RACE FEVER

Horse racing was a popular sport in Andover although the town itself never had an official racecourse. Eighteenth-century maps show a racecourse on Andover Down, but this was little more than a place where local owners matched their horses against each other, perhaps as an ancillary entertainment to the prize-fights held nearby at the Queen Charlotte. After one such race meeting in 1775 there was a ball at the Star and Garter Hotel – tickets were 3/– and tea was included.

Stockbridge Races began in 1775 and were very popular with the Andover gentry. The Bibury Club, probably the county's oldest racing club, transferred from Cleeve Hill, Cheltenham in 1831 to Stockbridge. The club, in its early days, had its headquarters in Andover at the Star and Garter (now Danebury Hotel), and was still there in 1859, as White's Directory testifies. There were racehorse training establishments at Danebury run by Young King of Stockbridge and by John Day of Danebury in Nether Wallop parish, both of which were held in high repute. Lord George Bentinck (1802-1848), one the country's greatest racing enthusiasts, had considerable interest in the Danebury stables and he was often in the area inspecting his horses and attending a race or two.

John Day's son, John Barnham Day, was himself an outstanding rider and was at one time jockey to King George IV. Day junior eventually took over as trainer at Danebury and his son, also a John Day, was an even more successful trainer, who in 1867 sent out 146 winners. One of his stable jockeys, Tom Cannon, married Day's daughter Kate in 1865 and later took over the stables and managed the racecourse.

Several locally trained horses went on to win the Derby and some of the local houses were named after these winners. The Cossacks in Stockbridge, originally a public house and drovers' meeting place, was renamed after the 1847 Derby winner. William Etwall, brother of the Andover MP Ralph Etwall, had a horse named Andover, which won the Derby in 1854. It was trained by John Day at the Danebury stables.

A sale-poster survives, albeit in a poor state, describing an auction of the rights to sell refreshments and to run the parking franchise at Stockbridge race meetings. Note the high cost of parking carriages and coaches on the racing enclosure:

STOCKBRIDGE RACES
17th, 18th, 19th, JUNE 1863.

To INNKEEPERS & Others:

TO BE LET, By Auction, by Mr. F. ELLEN,

At the GRAND STAND, on Stockbridge Race
Course,
On Tuesday, JUNE 9th, 1863, at two o'clock in
the afternoon.
1. The right of serving Refreshments in the
Grand Stand during the three days Races.
2. The whole of the Ground between the
Betting Enclosure and the Road, except a cer-
tain space near the Grand Stand and sufficient
approaches thereto, which will be reserved for
Carriages setting down and taking up at the
Grand Stand. The highest bidder for this Lot
will have the privilege of charging for all
Vehicles entering upon the ground let to him
at a rate not exceeding 3s. for each Coach,
Omnibus, Van, Break, Landau, Britzka, four-
wheel Cab, Chariot, or Fly ; 2s for each ordinary
four-wheel Phaeton, and 1s. each for two-wheel
Vehicles.
He will also be entitled to underlet the ground
for *Snuff-boxing Sticks*, &c."

(Snuff-boxing sticks were walking sticks with
snuff-boxes carved into their handles.)

During the weeks of the Stockbridge races, a
minstrel troupe would entertain visitors at the
town's hostelries, the town being full to over-
flowing for this great event. One of the country's
most famous jockeys during the nineteenth century was Fred Archer and whilst attending
Stockbridge races he would stay with his great
friend Billy Moon, a local benefactor and eccen-
tric, at Penton Lodge.

The last races at Stockbridge were in 1898,
when the Bibury Club transferred its allegiance
to the Salisbury Races. On the closure of the
course Tom Cannon purchased the Grosvenor
Hotel in Stockbridge where many relics of the
racecourse and the Day and Cannon families can
still be seen. Tom's great grandson is Lester
Piggott, the premier jockey of the 1970s and '80s.

One of the most illustrious visitors to the races
was Edward, Prince of Wales and later to be
Edward VII. He often stayed at Hermit Lodge in
Houghton Road and Lillie Langtry would often
be seen with him in the village.

77. *An 1875 map of the Danebury Down racecourse on which the Stockbridge Races were held.*

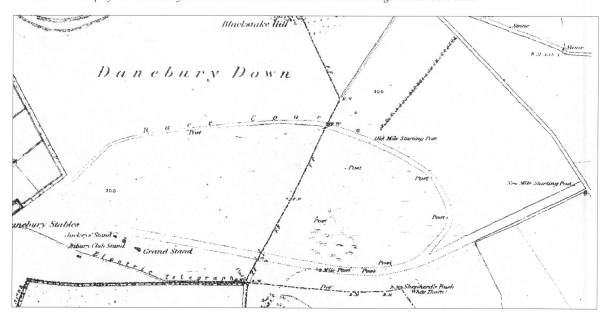

78. *Tom Cannon, one of the country's top jockeys and manager of the Danebury Racecourse. (Photo 1900).*

THE COMING OF THE RAILWAYS

Andover was a thriving market town in the 1840s on the main road to the West Country from London. The importance of Weyhill Fair, nearby, was well recognised and there was a need to get the produce etc. to the London markets quickly. This was recognised by the directors of the London & Southampton Railway and they built a large station at Micheldever, which opened on 11 March 1840. When it opened it was called Warren Farm, but soon after the name was changed to Andover Road.

The road to which the name referred was the old turnpike road or Galliker Way, which was a 10-mile journey from the station into the town. Galliker Way was one of the last turnpike roads in the county to be improved, primarily as a result of its importance to the town. The cutting

through Bere Hill, Andover, was one of the most impressive engineering feats of the turnpike era. The Ladies' Walk, a popular local footpath, crossed the route and Tasker and Fowle in 1851 erected a cast iron bridge to carry the path over the turnpike.

Despite the improvements to the road, the journey was a hard one, especially in the winter, and the town council petitioned for a more direct link to Basingstoke and beyond. The campaigning eventually paid off when the London & South Western Railway's line finally reached Andover in 1854. As a direct result of the new line opening, the Galliker Way turnpike took a huge drop in traffic and it never recovered. It remains a testimony to that early railway and turnpike history as Micheldever Road and the Iron Bridge, but is now stopped off at its junction with the modern A303 trunk road.

On 3 July 1854 the London & South Western Railway was opened at Andover and the contractor, Thomas Brassey, celebrated the occasion by bringing the directors of the line down from London in a special train, and treating them and local dignitaries to a feast. The line reached Salisbury three years later and in 1860 got to Exeter, putting Andover on an important mainline from London to the West of England.

The Andover Canal Railway Act was passed in 1858 allowing a railway to be built on or near the bed of the old canal from Andover to Redbridge (*see p54*), from where it joined the line from Southampton to Dorchester. At the Andover end it was connected to the line running to Basingstoke and London, and at Romsey it joined the line to Salisbury and Portsmouth. The new line opened in 1865. It was notorious for its sharp curves and rough ride, and was not improved until 1885 when the line was doubled.

The first stage of a link to Swindon was made when a line was opened to Marlborough in April of 1860. In 1872 local landowners projected a railway from Swindon to Andover utilising this stretch linking the GWR with the London & South Western Railway. It was known as the Swindon, Marlborough & Andover Railway and received its Act on 21 July 1873.

The Swindon section was built first, opening in July 1881; the southern section was completed on 21 March 1882, but a number of faults were found at Savernake and the Inspector decided they had to be corrected before he would give a certificate for passenger transit between Marlborough and Andover. Whilst this work was

79. Railways needed services as did turnpike roads. This watercolour is of Bishops Court House and Bridge Street c.1840. The area is today known as The Broadway. The turnpike gates and the Eight Bells Inn are to be seen – the inn later became the Station Hotel.

80. Micheldever Station c.1920. Originally known as Andover Road when it was opened in 1840.

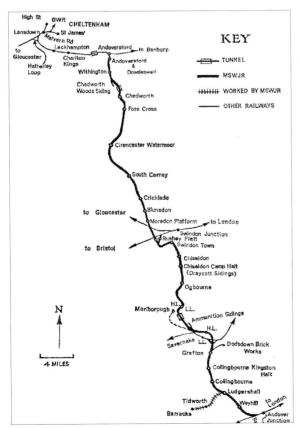

81. Andover Junction Station c.1900. The railway first reached Andover in 1854 and the station became a junction in 1882 with a line from Andover to Grafton.

82. A map of the railway from Cheltenham, through Andoversford to Andover, on completion in 1891.

going on the company reduced its losses by opening the line from Andover to Grafton. The first train on this section left Grafton on 1 May 1882 with the trains having to run over the London & South Western Railway line from Red Post Junction to Andover Junction.

By 1885 the Swindon, Marlborough and Andover Railway had reached Andover, but a further extension north of Swindon to Cheltenham was delayed until 1891 due to lack of funds. In 1884 the Midland & South Western Junction Railway came into being, and this time Andover station was renamed Andover Junction Station.

In 1900 the War Department built a branch off the line to service its Tidworth Camp and the Boer War traffic. This was closed to passengers on 17 September 1955 and the route through to Savernake was not used after 15 September 1958.

83. *A train leaving for Basingstoke in March 1963. Note the Andover Town loop in the foreground on the left.*

FOOTBALL

Andover Town Football Club was formed on 25 September 1883 at a public meeting held in Andover Guildhall. The first match was played on 27 October 1883 on Mr Stride's meadow (later known as the Walled Meadow) against Basingstoke Engineers. The *Andover Advertiser* reported on the match:

> The visitors displayed a marked inclination for obstreperousness and what was more to be regretted the Andover umpire's decision in language that was anything but gentlemanly .... we cannot too strongly condemn some of the language used. The Andover umpire was the headmaster of Andover Grammar School, the Rev. J.C. Witton.

The club's first four years were spent playing friendly matches until 1887 when the Hampshire League was formed. Andover played continuously in this, through both wars until 1968, the only club to do so. During their time in the league Andover won every trophy that the County Football Association had to offer.

THE SWIMMING BATH

For centuries the people of Andover had used the town river for many needs – drinking water, washing, waste water, water to drive machinery, mills etc. In 1865 the Council cleared an area of the river to permit safe bathing near the old gas works. The report in the *Andover Advertiser* in June that year reveals more:

> The arrangements for the new bath are now nearly complete and it will shortly be ready for public use. The committee have framed their rules so as to include all classes of swimmers. A first class subscription of 5s yearly will give access to the bath at all hours when it is open, together with the exclusive use of the dressing shed. A subscription of 2s 6d annually will admit to the general use of the bath but without the use of the dressing shed. For the benefit of persons who only require an occasional dip, penny tickets will be issued, but these will be only available during certain hours, namely from 12 to 3 in the day and from seven in the evening until dusk. On Saturdays the bath will be open to all bathers after 4 o'clock in the afternoon, and on Sundays to subscribers from six to eight in the morning. It must be admitted that the contractor, Mr Dance, has performed his work in the most satisfactory manner. Indeed, the clearness of the water, and the goodness of the bottom are surprising, considering the spot where the bath is constructed.

84. *The Andover Football Club team, late 1950s, winners of the Hampshire League.*

85. *The Walled Meadow c.1965, the home of the Andover Football Club until the Portway Stadium was built in the 1980s.*

THE POOR OF NEW STREET

The files of the *Andover Advertiser* record for us the state of the town through the years. On 6 May 1866 the newspaper notes:

> The Condition of New Street:
> Our attention has been directed to the moral condition of that unfortunate and unhealthy suburb, New Street. No one passing through it can fail to remark on the great number of children, many of them girls, who are idling around and playing about, without any education except in vice and depravity, and with no other prospect in life than misery and ruin. Our correspondent suggests that by bringing these facts prominently under the notice of the charitable and philanthropically disposed, something may be done to preserve young lives from contamination, and add to society a number of useful members.

The outcry or appeal for help through the *Advertiser* the following year had the desired effect and local philanthropists came forward to help build the New Street School and Lecture Hall. By 1869 the total of boys and girls in the school was 100, the average attendance was 69 and there was a Sunday School of about 55. For the following five years or so the school received good reports from the government inspectors, but in 1877 it received a very different verdict:

> The committee of this institution announced they are compelled to discontinue the day school hitherto carried on in the building, for want of funds, and not only so but a debt of £45 incurred in the past weeks remains unpaid; to defray this they solicit subscriptions. The discontinuance of the day school is much to be regretted as it has been doing really good work. Anything which tends to check the demoralising influence of the particular neighbourhood is worthy of encouragement. The building will still be used for Sunday School and other occasional purposes.

By 1891 the building was in such a sorry state of repair demolition was suggested and it was eventually the vicar's decision to remove it and to erect a school closer to the church, to become known as St Mary's Mission Hall.

THE FIRE BRIGADE

The first mention of a town Fire Brigade appears in 1838, when the new town council formed a committee to negotiate with a Mr Nurse, a Fire Office agent, for the purchase or hire of one of his engines. This might well have been the manually operated engine that resides now in the British Museum, in addition to about a dozen leather fire buckets. Back in 1717 the church-warden's accounts showed that an:

> Hingen be bought for the church and parish and one duzen of lether bu> cketts to be paid for at the expense of the parishenrs

In 1860 the council resolved that "…in future the expenses of the Parish Engine be defrayed from the Borough Rate instead of from the Church Rate" and at the same time formed the Fire Brigade Committee. The new committee immediately recommended that a more powerful engine be provided and that it be kept in a more accessible place than the engine-house in the churchyard at the rear of the Silent Man beerhouse at the top of the High Street.

A new engine arrived in 1868 and was housed in a shed adjacent to the Angel Inn at the top of the High Street. In 1877 the council was made responsible for the two parish fire engines.

The Andover Volunteer Fire Brigade was formed in 1867, comprising two companies. In 1879 fire hydrants were installed around the town. In 1880 the two engines still kept by the Angel Inn were moved to the urban sanitary authority's premises in East Street.

The Andover Town Brigade had a distinguished record of service until the Second World War, when the service structure was re-organised.

A NEW BADGE

One of the town's great benefactors and Mayor of Andover in 1871 was William Gue. He was due to represent the town at the opening of the International Exhibition in London that year, but looking at the chain of office, he was disappointed with its quality and commissioned a new one from solid gold with the Town Arms and engraved around it 'Mayor, Aldermen and Councillors of the Borough of Andover'. He presented it at a meeting of the council in 1871, saying that it was a disgrace to go to London half-clothed. On the reverse of the badge was the inscription "This chain and badge were presented to the Corporation of Andover, by William Gue, during his Mayoralty, 1871".

86. *The Adelaide Road Swimming Pool and Assembly Rooms in 1909. One of the first indoor pools in the south of England.*

AN INDOOR POOL

Following the success of the town's bathing area in the river, an indoor pool was built in 1885 in Adelaide Road by Frank Beale, who operated a builder's yard next door. The pool was one of the first of its kind in southern England. It also included hot slipper baths heated by a boiler fired by a large solid fuel furnace. The building itself was almost entirely built of wood with carved timber beams supporting a tiled roof. The walls were wood panelled and on one side of the pool were two small changing rooms and a ticket office. Mixed bathing was not allowed – the women having their own time between 11.15am and 12.30pm; the admission fee was 8d for women, a full 2d more than for men. In 1894 a fire razed the building to the ground. Beale set to work again and with remarkable speed the new building was back in business the next summer.

During the winter months the building doubled as Assembly Rooms for entertainment and there were many visiting players from all over the country. The business finally closed in 1975 and the land was bought by Test Valley District Council; the building itself was pulled down in 1976 to make way for a development of flats and a Health Centre.

87. *Aerial view over Andover taken on 9 May 1918 – note the site of Poore & Sons' brewery in the area behind the Guildhall.*

Fire and Riot

GREAT CHANGES

By 1900 great changes were happening in Bridge Street, as the large houses beside the White Hart Hotel were converted from residential to business use, and with the building of shop fronts on front gardens. The original building line can still be seen today if one looks above these shops. Cllr Pond occupied The Chestnuts, now the offices of Talbot Walker, solicitors. His stables and carriage house adjoined the river by the bridge – the Methodist Church later acquired that plot. The Methodists, previously in Winchester Street (in a building now occupied by the Salvation Army) from 1824, opened their new church on 19 April 1906.

On the site where 'Breakers' and Wilkinson's hardware shop now stand was a good looking house occupied by a veterinary surgeon named Gates. Next to this was a stonemason's yard and by that stood a small corn and coal merchant's office, run by T.H. Compton. Along from this was Hall's ginger-pop shop, which was later taken over by Colling & Tilling as a bicycle shop. The

next building was an office occupied by Reeke and where the Post Office now stands was an open yard and then a large private house, known as Western House, part of which can still be seen through the gates to the Post Office yard.

On the far side of the level crossing is the area known as the Broadway and on the site where Kennedy's builders' supplies stood (now sadly boarded up), was a grand house known as Bishop's Court. It was covered in japonica and occupied by one of the town's magistrates, a Mr Kellow. It is believed that it stood on the site of the administrative building of a medieval leper colony of St Mary Magdalene. Over the road was, and still is, the Station Hotel. This building predates the railway and was once known as the Eight Bells but also by many similar names relating to the number of bells then installed at the nearby church.

There were very few houses in Vigo Road beyond St John's Road before 1905. These included Batchelor's Barn and the Pest House. Most of the land in that area was at that time owned by the Dance and Herbert families, and more houses there were built between 1907 and 1909.

88. *The brewery of Poore & Sons c.1900. The offices were in the High Street behind the Guildhall.*

89. *Bridge Street, c.1911.*

90. *The Methodist church in Bridge Street, shortly after it opened in 1906.*

ANDOVER CO-OPERATIVE

The Andover Co-operative Society began in 1900 at the home of Mr Wellesley Thorne in Victoria Park (off Junction Road). A later meeting was held in Foresters' Hall, London Street on 20 December 1900, which some 175 people attended, and where the Society was formally constituted. The Society's first shop was in New Street, managed by a Mr R. Aspin, and some good progress enabled it to move into larger premises in Bridge Street by the end of 1901. At the move the membership stood at 400 and profits amounted to £122.

In 1905 land became available opposite, on the corner of Town Mills Road and Bridge Street, and the Society bought it for £2,500. When the leases of the adjacent properties, the Catherine Wheel coffee house and a cycle shop, expired the Co-op acquired them as well and used the opportunity to rebuild completely. The President, E. A. Mills, officially opened the new building in 1923. The Co-op was a feature of Bridge Street shopping and well liked by the Town Development newcomers in the mid 1960s. The Society was taken over by the Portsea Island Co-operative Society in the 1960s and the store was rebuilt again in the mid 1970s, incorporating a hairdresser's and a restaurant overlooking the river. Property prices began to rise however and the Society decided to cut its losses: the Andover Co-op closed its doors on 16 August 1986.

THE GREAT FIRE OF NEW STREET

A disastrous fire occurred in 1901 involving a large number of thatched cottages in New Street. The event was reported in national newspapers, with the *Daily Graphic* devoting considerable space to line drawings of the destruction, though the report caused some resentment by referring to Andover as a Hampshire 'village'.

The fire began in a barn at the rear of a row of cottages at around 11.30pm on Easter Sunday, 8 April. A police officer saw the smoke but before he had a chance to raise the alarm, the fire had developed. The flames, fanned by a stiff breeze, soon jumped the cartway by the barn and the Blacksmith's Arms was well alight before the occupants realised their predicament. The landlady, on attempting to secure the cashbox from her bedroom, was forced back by dense smoke and within thirty seconds the room was in flames.

The fire engulfed sheds and houses near Cook's Farm. The roof of a blazing barn fell in, scattering burning thatch in all directions, and a large section fell on Ball's Cottages (numbers 111-125 New Street), which were very soon in flames. It was only seconds later when the fire spread to March's cottages and to Steven's Bakery on the other side. When the hoses arrived the lower end of New Street was an avenue of fire and as other firemen turned up with the manual engine March's cottages were soaked with water to prevent flames

91. *A large procession was held in Andover to mark the wedding of the Duke and Duchess of York (later George V and Queen Mary) on 6 July 1893. The theme was Andover's Trade and Prosperity, so there were many trade cars and tableaux. This one is the Andover Co-operative Society's entry and is advertising CWS cigars.*

92. *The river in front of Town Mills c.1900. The carriers are watering their horses before continuing work.*

93. *New Street c.1900 before the fire. Note the many thatched cottages to the right.*

94. *The scene in New Street after the Great Fire on Easter Sunday, 8 April 1901.*

95. *The Great Fire of Andover as depicted in The Graphic in 1901.*

96. *Andover Junction station during the great snowstorm on 25 April 1908.*

going beyond the thatch. The fire was fought for two hours and by daybreak it was seen that 17 homes, the Blacksmith's Arms and farm buildings were destroyed, leaving 80-100 people homeless.

Mr P. Bloxham of London Street made available two of his malthouses to take some of the families, and the Mission Room in New Street was turned into a temporary shelter, while others had to go to the Union Workhouse. The Blacksmith's Arms was rebuilt shortly afterwards but it was some 80 years before the void left by this fire was again built on. A steam-powered fire engine, due for delivery one month before the fire happened, arrived in May of that year.

THE BETA AIRSHIP

The military airship *Beta* had to make a forced landing at Little Park near Anna Valley on 13 July 1910 during a flight from Farnborough to Salisbury Plain. It flew very low over the town and townspeople ran out into the streets to watch it pass overhead. From Little Park it was towed by ropes across country by soldiers, over the trees and telegraph wires to the quarry at Anna Valley, near Tasker's of Andover where Mr Roe (of Roe's Garage, Charlton Road) repaired its broken crankshaft.

The airship had a capacity of 35,000 cu ft and was powered by a Green engine. It could be claimed that it was the first truly efficient British service airship. However after her maiden flight on 26 May 1910, she was subject to many modifications including the fitting of wireless. Despite her success, a complete reconstruction was undertaken in 1912. When she emerged she was almost a different airship, and was henceforth known as *Beta II*. The airship was taken off active duty in 1916, but the gondola survives in the Science Museum, South Kensington.

THE ANDOVER RIOTS

In June 1914, Andover was the scene of serious street disturbances, following an unpopular paternity award in the local court. Vivian Robert Isidore Harvey, the son of Frederick and Sarah Harvey who owned three businesses in the High Street, was accused of being the father of the child of their servant girl Phyllis Beckingham. Vivian denied that the boy, born on 31 December the previous year, was his and so Beckingham and her mother petitioned the local magistrates for an affiliation order to be granted naming him as the father. The magistrates decided there was insufficient proof and the case was lost. What made matters worse was that in another case on

97. *A military airship, the Beta, made a forced landing at Little Park, Anna Valley on 13 July 1910, and was towed by soldiers and volunteers to the quarry nearby where Mr Roe repaired the crankshaft.*

the same day an order was made against a railway worker named in a similar case, leading to claims that there was one law for the poor and another for the rich and that the magistrates were all friends of Vivian Harvey.

The two women tried again later to bring a case before the magistrates but it met with the same answer. Outside the courthouse there was much jeering and jostling and the Beckinghams, urged on by the crowd, physically attacked Harvey who took out a summons for assault against them. The case came before the local magistrates on 8 June 1914. The women were both fined but refused to pay, whereupon they were sentenced to a short spell in prison instead. After a few days their fine was paid by supporters and the two women were released early. The Beckinghams arrived back in Andover at 9.40 pm to a crowd at the town station around two thousand strong, some of whom were armed with sticks, stones and tin cans. The throng then paraded along Bridge Street to the High Street to demonstrate outside the Harvey shops.

There were only three policemen on duty that night and not knowing what to do with a gathering of this size positioned themselves outside the shops. The crowd began banging sticks and cans together making a deafening sound. Suddenly the sound stopped and a stone was thrown that went straight through the shop window of 78 High Street. A huge cheer arose and more missiles smashed windows. Sergeant Every made his way to a phone box and called for reinforcements, but it was not until after midnight that they arrived. The fire brigade was called, as it was feared the crowd might set fire to shops. Arthur Beale, the Fire Chief, connected the hose to a nearby stand pipe intending to turn it on the mob, but no-one would give the OK to do so. The crowd then turned on the firemen and tipped over the hose cart and rendered the hose useless. The Mayor, W. Percival Clarke, intervened and tried reasoning with the ringleaders, to no avail. There was discussion whether the Riot Act should be read, but this was not done.

Peace was only restored when police reinforcements arrived from Winchester. The Hampshire Constabulary fielded fifty sergeants and constables to quell the affray but despite their presence the crowd refused to disperse until force was used against them. The riot was described as "one of the roughest ever known in the annals of the

98. Vigo Road Recreation Ground, June 1911. The mayor and mayoress, Mr and Mrs J. Compton Reeks, planted an oak to commemorate the coronation of George V. Astride a horse is Mr F. Beale, who led the carnival procession.

Hampshire Constabulary, the police relying on the old English style of fighting with clenched fist".

By morning much of the night's troubles had subsided but the town was described as resembling "a Dublin Street after a riot." Tension was still high and during the Saturday extra police were brought in from Basingstoke, Winchester, Southampton and Aldershot as well as mounted police, stabled at the Junction Hotel, near the station. Crowds began to congregate at about 10pm and when more people arrived from New Street some resorted to vandalism when they began smashing the windows of Charles Howard the photographer and Rolls the Butcher. The Mayor was in the High Street that night in case he was required to read the Riot Act, but again this was not done. The police stepped in with fists and truncheons flying yet again and bit-by-bit the rioters subsided but not before they had smashed many windows and street lamps in the Upper High Street and New Street; in Charlton

Road they threatened the Junction Hotel until the horses' stables there were removed to the local police station.

On the Sunday a much smaller crowd appeared in the High Street, but the police were easily able to deal with them and the riot was quashed. Throughout the whole event only one arrest was made – of a man who was caught red-handed smashing a window, but when it came to court, the house owner refused to prosecute and the case was dismissed.

Vivian Harvey refused to admit he was the father of the child to the end of his life in 1978.

100. *The Rothsay Hotel at Weyhill was turned into a military hospital during the First World War. This photograph was taken c.1918.*

During the war the Rothsay Hotel at Weyhill was turned into a military hospital and at the time of the surrender in 1918 the *Andover Advertiser* on 29 November noted that there were 24 patients receiving treatment and that gifts had been received from E. Wigan Esq. (grapes and apples), Mrs Gould (apples) Mrs Harmer (vegetables) and Mrs Quale (Union Jack).

LOFT WORSHIP

By 1915 the population of Andover was around 8,000. There were some Catholics among them, but not many, and Mass was celebrated in the loft of a small barn at the rear of the Station Hotel in Bridge Street. This remained their meeting hall

101. *The barn at the rear of the Station Hotel in Bridge Street, used as a Catholic meeting hall from 1915 to 1920. (Photo 2001)*

99. *The Parliamentary election of 1906. Capt. Walter V. Faber was elected MP for West Hampshire division, which included Andover. The poll was declared at Andover Guildhall and the address to his supporters was held at the Star and Garter in the High Street (see above). The Faber family owned a brewery at Weyhill, later sold off to Strong & Co. based at Romsey.*

THE DRILL HALL

The foundation stone of the Drill Hall in East Street was laid on 2 October 1908 by General Sir Ian Hamilton and was ready in time for its official opening by the Lord Lieutenant of Hampshire, the Marquis of Winchester, on 21 October 1908. It was built under the requirements of the Territorial and Reserve Act of 1907 and immediately became home to a number of units of Volunteers and Yeomanry. The Hall was the first of a generation of new TA Drill Halls in the county. It was built of steel and timber framing, with a concrete base and tower and covered externally by corrugated iron.

At the outbreak of the First World War the Hall became extremely important being much in demand as a muster point for numerous units.

102. *St John the Baptist Roman Catholic church, opened in Croye Close in 1958. (Photo: 1992).*

A CELEBRATION

Shortly after the war in 1919 the residents of New Street formed a committee to celebrate the signing of the peace treaty between the Allies and Germany. Preparations took several weeks during which collections were made to finance the events planned. To the women of 'the street', as it was affectionately named, it was the end of four years of hardship, anxiety and dread caused by the absence of their men fighting in the battlefields of Europe. To the men it was relief that they would no longer be required to wake up in the trenches.

Highlight of the 'Joy Day', was to be a grand parade led by the band of the Hampshire Regiment, but a rail strike meant that they could not come and the New Street Jazz Band was moved up the parade to take their place. The children spent that morning transforming the normally drab street into a blaze of colour using flags and decorations they had prepared the previous day. The parade began outside the Grammar School and ended in March's meadow, where a fairground topped the celebrations.

Two women and two girls bearing the inscription "Thanks to those who helped to end the war"

until 1920 when temporary accommodation was found in Weyhill Road. A new church dedicated to St John the Baptist was erected in Croye Close in 1958. The Missionaries of the Company of Mary, often known as the Montfort Missionaries, a religious congregation of Missionary Priests and Brothers founded in France in 1716, look after the present church, which was extended in 1987.

103. *New Street 'Joy Day' in 1919. Preparations for the march to celebrate the signing of the peace treaty.*

104. *The Cenotaph in place outside the Guildhall c.1928. It remained there until 1956, when it was moved to a new Garden of Remembrance created in the old churchyard at Andover.*

105. *The building that was once Andover's power station in Anton Mill Road. It is now used as a tyre and exhaust centre. (Photo: 2001)*

carried a banner. Fifteen archways of flags spanned the street as the parade wended its way. Heavy rain ended the proceedings but no one was daunted.

THE MEMORIALS
Soon after the end of hostilities, Andover decided to erect a war memorial and also a new hospital in memory of the fallen. Subscriptions were sought and as part of the fund raising, bricks for the hospital were sold for 3d each. Meanwhile, a temporary memorial was placed in lower High Street, which was the scene of the town's first Armistice Service in 1919. In May 1920, the Lieutenant of Hampshire, Maj-Gen the Rt. Hon. J.E.B. Seeley, unveiled a permanent memorial just outside the forecourt of the Guildhall. Capt. H.R. Cowley designed it, and the work was done by Mr Harry Page at his Angel Yard works; it was inscribed with the names of 213 men from Andover, Enham and Smannell.

The memorial is the only one in the country to bear the dates of the Great War as 1914-1920, the reason being that men from Andover were sent with the Hampshire Regiment to Russia to fight alongside the anti-Bolsheviks in Murmansk. They saw some action and sustained about a dozen casualties, holding out until February 1920. The cenotaph was moved to its present site in St Mary's churchyard in 1956 after repeated representations that considerable desecration took place on market days when the steps to it were strewn with empty boxes and garbage.

THE POWER STATION
Edwards & Armstrong, a company from Stroud in Gloucestershire, which had built numerous power stations all over the West Country through the 1920s, built Andover power station in 1926. Normally the main source of power was the steam turbine, but the Andover station was very small and they chose to use a diesel generator, made by W.H. Allen & Co Ltd. of Bedford and of a type used in many of the ocean liners of the day. The actual engine used was the same one as had been on Allen's stand in the Palace of Engineering at the British Empire Exhibition at Wembley in 1924.

The electricity was supplied to the town area – High Street, Bridge Street and London Street – by means of underground cables, but areas outside of this were supplied on poles because of the cost of laying the cables. By 1929 the poles had extended up Weyhill Road to the railway line, Salisbury Road and Mead Road, up London Road and as far as the cricket ground and along Winchester Road to the top of the hill.

The power station's life was to be a short one for the same year it opened the Government passed an Act setting up a state financed Central Electricity Board to construct and run a National Grid of high voltage power lines. The power station ceased to generate the town's supply in 1931 when Andover was connected to the Grid. However the power station remained able to supply power up until 1950, being used from time to time as a supplementary supply. The building, in Anton Mill Lane, is now used as a tyre and exhaust centre.

106. *Andover war memorial after it was moved to its new site in St Mary's churchyard in 1956. In its previous position in front of the Guildhall it was unveiled by the Prince of Wales in 1923.*

FIRE AT McDOUGALL'S

In the early hours of the morning of 19 August 1925 the McDougall's flourmill near Junction Station caught fire. One of the town's landmarks, the three-storied building containing valuable machinery was completely gutted. The fire brigade arrived after 2am when they could do little to save the main building. The packing rooms were rescued however and the workers arriving for the morning shift were able to carry on as usual packing the flour for transmission to its customers by rail.

It was not long before the mill was rebuilt and it remains to this day one of the town's most prominent features. Its rebuilding provided the opportunity to re-equip the mill and to install electrically-powered machinery, now that the town was able to generate its own power.

Henry Fiander, who formerly owned Anton Mill, originally erected the mill in 1905, before it was acquired by McDougalls Ltd.

THE CHAMBER OF TRADE

The Andover and District Chamber of Trade was formed in April 1923 with Percival Clarke as its first president. Many times over the early years the Chamber campaigned for new industry to come to the town until the signing of the Town Development agreement in 1961. In 1937 they discussed the possibility of a bypass for Andover, but as we know it was not until many years later this came to fruition. After the Second World War the Chamber took a keen interest in the development of the town and they joined with the Andover Trades Council to form a joint industrial committee, with a view to attracting more businesses. Development problems took up a great deal of the Chamber's time and in the mid 1970s they found it necessary to split into three groups covering industry, business and professions, and retail and distribution.

Two large printing concerns moved into the area. Kelly's Directories Limited from Kingston upon Thames chose Andover in 1932 when they needed to develop their expanding business. The Chapel River Press moved into Weyhill Road, remaining there for many years before being amalgamated with McCorquodale Printers, printing magazines and comics; they moved to the Portway Industrial Estate in the 1980s.

107. Weyhill Road looking toward the Round House and the Salisbury Road junction c.1910.

108.   Weyhill Road at its junction with The Avenue, c.1912.

109.   Upper High Street c.1923. Howard & Sons (artists' materials and photographer) is in the foreground on the left-hand side. Scott's Shoe Shop is on the right between Harvey's and Pond's.

110. *Souvenir programme for the George V Silver Jubilee celebrations, 6 May 1935.*

111. *Advertisement for a 'really hot bath' at the swimming pool in London Road.*

MORE FIRES

In May 1935 another disastrous fire took place in New Street when the imposing Etwall House was severely damaged. The Moore Hall was later built on this site and only demolished in June 1990 to make way for a doctor's surgery. Yet another fire a year later left eighteen people homeless when four cottages burnt down on what is now the site of the Merrie Monk public house.

SILVER JUBILEE

The Silver Jubilee of King George V, on 6 May 1935, was celebrated by a procession beginning at the recreation ground in Vigo Road, around the town and back to the Walled Meadow in London Street. The band of the 4th Co. Territorials did the March Past and the Mayor, Cllr Borseberry Shaw Porter, took the salute. There was a grand party on the Meadow for all the schoolchildren, who were presented with Jubilee mugs by the Mayoress. The festivities continued into the evening with dancing in the High Street to music by the Andover Town Band. There was also a late evening dance in the Drill Hall to the music of Ivor Buckland and his Blue Bohemians. Miss Sonia Shaw Porter lit the customary Monster Bonfire at 10pm at the top of Old Winton Road. Two days earlier there had been a tea for the older citizens of the town where they were presented with a souvenir gift of tea.

A NEW POOL

In 1936 the Lido open-air swimming pool was opened in the Walled Meadow, London Street, next to where Andover's present fire station stands. It also provided hot bath facilities but about a year after the new indoor pool was opened at Cricklade in 1975 the Lido closed.

War and Peace

THE STORM CLOUDS

The storm clouds of war began to loom during the early months of 1938. Throughout the whole of that year ARP (Air Raid Precautions) meetings were held in Andover and the villages of the district. Wardens were appointed and First Aid Posts and Wardens' Posts sited; gas mask training was given and the provision of shelters was discussed. Every home in the country was issued with a booklet *The Protection of the Home Against Air Raids*. During September, 40,000 gas masks for the town and rural areas of Andover, Kingsclere and Whitchurch were distributed from Clare House in East Street (now the Central Club).

During the year work also commenced on building Barton Stacey Army Camps and Middle Wallop airfield; at the same time Perham Down and Tidworth Garrisons were enlarged. Hope and confidence grew during the winter that peace might win through, but optimism was utterly shattered in March 1939, when Hitler's army first marched on defenceless Czechoslovakia and then on Lithuania.

PREPARATIONS

Civil Defence organisations, manned by volunteers, trained new recruits and the public about 'what to do in the event of war'. The early part of 1939 was a busy time for the ARP service in Andover, which held repeated exercises. Lt. Col. F.L. Congreve, DSP, MC, of Abbotts Ann took over as controller at Clare House. In fact Clare House was the only building prepared for air raids during the first week of the war. Sandbags were piled high around the building and tape criss-crossed the windows.

A full-scale dummy exercise (on paper only) was carried out in March 1939, when bombers carried out a 'night attack' on the town. ARP services were called upon to deal with high explosives, incendiary bombs, and mustard and phosgene gas. The newspapers reported that all acquitted themselves well.

A St John's Ambulance Brigade was formed in Andover in 1938. Its inaugural meeting was on 11 July 1939 and the brigade worked closely with the local Red Cross Society and held first aid classes for the public and newly recruited members. In addition, the British Red Cross Society had four active detachments in the Andover area during 1940-45. Both organisations held courses

118. Clare House, East Street, became the home of the Civil Defence and ARP during the Second World War. Sandbags were piled high around the building. It now houses the Central (working men's) Club. (Photo: 2001)

119. *Priory Hall, home of the St John's Ambulance Brigade, with Wolversdene House in the background. This was the Home Guard Club during the Second World War.*

at Clare House for members of the local Civil Defence and ARP, and others were held in local villages. Fundraising too was important and the St John's Ambulance Brigade joined forces with the British Red Cross Society to collect money for the Prisoners of War Comfort Fund in December 1944.

As Barton Stacey received the first of the militiamen, plans were in hand to build Chilbolton and Thruxton airfields. Shelters were built around the town in the event of an air raid and they were also provided at the Walled Meadow and there were four in Bridge Street, each capable of accommodating fifty people.

120. *Queen Elizabeth stopped at the Municipal Offices in Bridge Street on 23 July 1939, en route to review the Queen's Bays, a cavalry regiment, at Tidworth. The mayor, Alderman W.J. Armstead, greeted her.*

Andover Air Raid Precautions

A FIRST AID CLASS

Will commence at CLARE HOUSE for
BEGINNERS on
THURSDAY, JANUARY 4th, 1940, at 7,45 p.m.
At the end of the Course of Lectures an Examination for the 1st Year's St. John Ambulance Brigade Certificate will be arranged.

VOLUNTEERS ARE VERY URGENTLY REQUIRED FOR FIRST AID PARTIES AND FOR THE MUTUAL ASSISTANCE FIRST AID PARTY REQUIRED UNDER THE COUNTY SCHEME

Also   WOMEN   AMBULANCE   DRIVERS
WANTED

**Resident in Andover. Drivers must be available
for Duty Day or Night**
APPLY TO CLARE HOUSE BETWEEN 9.30 a.m.
and 5 p.m.

121. *Advertisement for First Aid classes at Clare House, 1940.*

THE QUEEN'S VISIT

Queen Elizabeth made a brief stop in the town on 23 July 1939 on her way to visit the Queen's Bays, a cavalry regiment at Tidworth. She was met by the Mayor, Alderman W. J. Armstead, outside the Municipal Offices. Crowds lined Bridge Street to witness her arrival. A British Paramount newsreel was made of the event and survives to record the event for posterity.

FIRST EFFECTS

After the declaration of war in September, all the preparations of the Borough Council and the ARP were activated. A Fire Guard was formed and regular fire watching began. There were only one or two daylight air raid warnings at this stage.

The first real effects were felt on Friday 1 September 1939 when there was an influx of some 1,000 children and some mothers and fathers, evacuated from Southampton, Portsmouth and other South Coast areas. The dispersal centre was Andover Grammar School, from where they were sent out to private houses in town and villages. The pupils of Itchen Grammar School in Southampton were among those evacuated to Andover in September 1939 and they shared accommodation with Andover Grammar School until Christmas 1944. Boys from both these schools built six air raid shelters in the school's football field.

On 13 September 1939 the *Andover Advertiser* reported that there were 678 evacuees in the town

122. The long and short of it – M.J.T. Crang and R.M. Gilbert in their Civil Defence-ARP uniforms.

BOROUGH OF ANDOVER

EMERGENCY POWERS (DEFENCE) ACTS
1939 AND 1940

REQUISITION OF UNNECESSARY RAILINGS

Under direction by the Minister of Supply all unnecessary iron or steel railings, posts, chains, bollards, gates, stiles, etc., in the Borough of Andover will shortly be removed and collected for use in the national war effort in iron and steel works and foundries.

Under the provisions of Regulation 50, paragraph (3A) of the Emergency Powers (Defence) General Regulations no person shall be liable, by virtue of any obligation imposed by any lease or other instrument affecting the land or by or under any enactment or otherwise to replace or provide a substitute for the thing severed, or to pay any sum by way of damages or penalty or to suffer any forfeiture in consequence of a failure to perform any such obligation, and any person who has guaranteed the performance of any such obligation shall be correspondingly relieved of his liability under the guarantee.

Dated this 26th January, 1942.

Municipal Offices,   E. J. O. Gardiner,
    Andover.   *Town Clerk.*

It is hoped that owners will be prepared to make a free gift of their railings etc., to the nation, but property owners and others whose interests are affected by the removal and who desire to claim compensation may obtain the appropriate form from:

The Borough Surveyor, Municipal Offices,
Bridge Street, Andover.

Under the provisions of the Compensation (Defence) Act, 1939, no claim for compensation ordinarily can be entertained unless notice of claim has been given to the appropriate authority within a period of six months from the date of removal of the railings, etc.

123. Emergency Order requisitioning iron railings for the war effort, 1942.

area. A complete blackout of all property was ordered and petrol-rationing books were introduced on 16 September, in preparation for full rationing on the 22nd. Before that the *Advertiser* reported that "all motorists were striving to hoard petrol and were calling at all pumps in turn". Identity cards were made obligatory.

THE LDV AND THE HOME GUARD

The Local Defence Volunteers (LDV) were formed on 14 May 1940. On that day Churchill's new War Secretary, Anthony Eden, spoke on the radio about the threat of German parachutists and called for large numbers of men between the ages of 17 and 65 to come forward to offer their services. Within 24 hours a quarter of a million men were enlisted. The Volunteers were later put under the auspices of the Army and the title changed to that of the Home Guard on 23 July 1940.

The 1st Battalion (Andover) Home Guard operated in an area covering some 360 sq. miles and was divided into eight companies with a total strength of 1600 men. Col. G.E. Millner, DSO, OBE, MC was the commanding officer and Lieut-Col. H.R. Currie (then Major), his second in command. It operated from the Drill Hall in East Street and it was there that several dances and other functions were held to raise funds to aid the war effort. Approximately £8000 was collected in this way of which £3000 went towards the Hampshire Prisoner of War Fund. Some funds were used to start the Home Guard Club, which after the war became the Wolversdene Club.

One of the Battalion's main duties was the running of a battle-training course at Fullerton where RAF men were trained alongside the Home Guard. Many high-ranking officials had demonstrations specially arranged for them including one for Field Marshal Montgomery.

124. *The Civil Defence wardens for North Western Area, Andover, probably a group photograph for distribution after hostilities ceased.*

RATIONING

The town's market was moved from the High Street to the Walled Meadow, but after only a short time this proved too wet and it was moved again to the Corporation Yard in Bridge Street, now the car park at the rear of the Iceland Freezer Centre. Here it remained throughout the war, not returning to the High Street until 1948. Rationing began on 8 September 1939 with the weekly allowance per person being 4oz of bacon or ham, 4oz butter, 12oz sugar.

A new telephone exchange was opened in 1940 – then ranked as the most up-to-date exchange in the country. No other exchanges were built during the war years as most of the other telecommunications equipment and machinery was made for export and war use.

CENSORSHIP

In 1940 came press censorship, in which all newspaper articles relating to enemy attacks etc. had to be vetted by government officials at the Ministry of Information local office at Reading.

On 10 January in Andover, 23 voluntary women ambulance drivers went on strike over the shock-

ing condition of the vehicles they had to drive. Replacement vehicles were quick to arrive.

The first reports of casualties and prisoners appeared in the columns of the *Advertiser*. In April RAF Middle Wallop opened as the 15th Flying Training School. As it was thought that Tidworth would be a likely German target, no further evacuees were received there. On Sunday 26 May, the Dunkirk evacuation began. By the 29th, 47,300 troops had been rescued from Dunkirk, by the 31st, 68,000, and by the 3rd June, when the last ships left Dunkirk, a total of 338,226 men had been brought back. Soon after, seven trains pulled into Tidworth crammed with survivors of the evacuation.

THE BATTLE OF BRITAIN

In Andover during June 1940, the Air Raid Sirens sounded at night for the first time in war.

The Germans, with their new forward base, stepped up bombing attacks on Britain, and during the period 10 July - 31 October Britain put up virtually every aircraft that could fly to defend the country. Docks, Channel shipping and air-

125. *Andover ARP Rescue and Demolition men and van in 1940.*

fields were attacked and London blitzed. On 14 July 1940, nine bombs were dropped near Clanville – four cows were killed and a cottage was damaged, but there were no civilian casualties. That month 500 more evacuees arrived from the Portsmouth area.

On 13 August, German aircraft bombed RAF Andover; in all ten bombs were dropped, hitting the airfield, parade ground and the squadron headquarters block. Three personnel were killed, one injured, and six aircraft on the ground damaged. Bombs also fell near the Andover War Memorial Hospital and at the top of The Avenue, but there was no damage.

The next day, the wireless station at Weyhill was bombed and two were killed. Twelve Junkers 88 aircraft bombed Middle Wallop, where a hangar was badly damaged; three men were killed and three Blenheim fighters destroyed on the ground.

On 23 August a number of incendiary bombs were dropped at Little London and Woodhouse. One fell through the roof of the Wells family home and burst into flame beside the bed of two young boys. The fire was quickly extinguished and no one was hurt. During August and September more incendiary bombs fell, two on Andover gasworks. Several fell at Goodworth Clatford causing slight damage to property.

MORE ATTACKS ON THE AIRFIELD

On 26 March 1941 Andover airfield was raided again; this time by a single Junkers 88, which dropped eight bombs but released them too low and the fuses did not go off. Ground gunners brought down the aircraft and it crashed at Eastover, Abbotts Ann. A night raid was made on the airfield on 7 April when twenty bombs were dropped. Three people were killed and another was seriously injured. On 16 April 1941, seven bombs were again dropped on the airfield; this time there were no casualties, but serious damage was done to property including the NAAFI.

FUNDRAISING

The Andover Spitfire Fund was set up in September 1940 and raised over £3,500 by the end of the year. In October a German Messerschmitt aircraft was displayed in the High Street and later at the rear of the Savoy Cinema in London Street.

During War Weapons Week in 1941 the town raised a total of £204,026 – a sum equivalent to £9.50 per head of population. News came of the sinking of *HMS Hood* on which a number of local men were serving and who went down with the ship. Andover & District Warship Week was held in March 1942 and £214,467 was raised. The Admiralty advised the town that *HMS Nestor*, an N Class destroyer, would be Andover's adopted ship. Unfortunately the ship was sunk in June 1942 when in action in the Mediterranean and consequently the plaque commemorating the adoption could not be awarded; it resides today in Andover Museum.

126. Wings for Victory Campaign, May 1943. Andover raised £232,788 for the war effort.

127. Souvenir programme for Andover's 'Aid to Russia Week' in 1942.

ANDOVER'S AID TO RUSSIA WEEK
SEPTEMBER 11th—SEPTEMBER 20th, 1942

WITH YOUR AID
THEY NEED NOT DIE

RAF LONGPARISH

The railway line from the junction with the LSWR at Hurstbourne to the junction with the Andover/ Southampton line at Fullerton had further work done to it during 1942 in order to service an RAF camp that had been set up in Harewood Forest to act as an ammunition depot. The camp (RAF Longparish) housed No 202 Maintenance Unit and contained a number of small huts used for the storage of bombs and bullets. The huts were linked to the railhead by concrete roads many of which are used today as footpaths.

At one time fifteen mobile cranes were engaged in loading and unloading bombs ranging in size from 500 lb. to the 4000 lb. blockbusters. It has been estimated that over 6000 wagons of bombs were stored at the camp during the build-up to D Day. On 28 July a number of incendiary bombs were dropped on the town but all were quickly extinguished by the ARP services. During preparations for the Normandy landings some seventy special trains carried troops, arms and supplies to military areas on Marlborough Downs and Tidworth. Savernake Forest was turned into an ammunition dump in preparation for the big day.

On 5 July 1944 came the first of two disasters when an American Flying Fortress, coming into land, clipped the top of Burbidge's bakery in Weyhill Road and plunged into a field killing pigs and severely damaging houses in Ashfield Road, setting one on fire. The American crew of four were killed but miraculously no civilians were injured. Ten days later a stray V1 flying bomb crashed into houses, a school and the Royal Oak public house at Goodworth Clatford. Six people killed in the pub had all come to the area to avoid the London Blitz.

The Home Guard was stood down on 3 December 1944 when more than 7000 representative members from every part of the country gathered in London for the final parade before the King, who took the salute in Hyde Park. Local parades took place in almost every town and village of Britain to mark the occasion.

On 8 May 1945 the war with Germany ended and VE celebrations began all over the town with church parades, street parties and the like. The *Advertiser* reported lists of returning servicemen and the battle honours they had received.

128. The Band of H Company, Andover Home Guard, c.1944.

129.   *A street party in Windsor Road, 8 May 1945, to celebrate VE Day.*

EARLY POST WAR HAPPENINGS

Andover had been a police division since the formation of the Hampshire Constabulary, but in 1947 this privilege was removed. Ironically that year the incidence of crime in the district and the percentage of detections was the highest ever known.

Andover Borough Council purchased the spacious mansion Beech Hurst in Weyhill Road in 1947 for use as Corporation offices. The Ratepayers' Association considered this a serious extravagance and sent a deputation to the Finance Committee meeting in the Guildhall. The skill of the chairman, Alderman R. Charlton, systematically dealt with each of the protests in turn, giving them a lengthy explanation of the necessity of extending the administration facilities, and he won the day.

A FLAME IN ANDOVER

The Olympic Games of 1948 were held at Wembley in London and the yachting events were held at Torquay in Devon. The Olympic torch was brought by relay runners drawn from HM Forces

130.   *The Olympic Flame being brought through Andover en route to the yacht regatta at Torquay, 1948.*

to the Torquay regatta through Andover, where it was handed over to a local runner, Flt-Lt D M Brown, a member of the Andover Athletic Club, who ran with it through London Street and Bridge Street, up Western Road to the Salisbury Road and out to Anna Valley. Here he handed it over to one of two Bournemouth runners, who took it as far as Lopscombe Corner at the Wiltshire border.

131. The first elected Andover Carnival Queen, Mary Fluen, in 1952. Her attendants were Iris Beezer, Janet Shadwell and Sheila Rawlings.

New Blood

In 1953 Andover celebrated the coronation of Elizabeth II with a week long programme of events beginning on 30 May, with a Young Farmers' Club Rally and Gymkhana at the Walled Meadow, and later a dance at the TA Centre in East Street. There were street parties in the town and all children up to the age of 15 received a souvenir mug, whilst pensioners received a canister of tea. At 7.30pm a tableaux representing events in the history of Andover wound through the town. There was dancing in the High Street from 9pm and later a torchlight procession led by the members of Andover Round Table to the Golf Course, where a bonfire was lit by the mayor.

The festivities concluded with a concert by the band of the Royal Electrical and Mechanical Engineers at the Vigo Road Recreation Ground. Andover celebrated again only a month later when the mayor welcomed the actor and actress couple Michael Denison and Dulcie Gray to open the Andover Carnival.

ANTI-FLUORIDATION

The Ministry of Health in 1955 asked Andover to participate in a scheme to study the effects of fluoride on public health, one of four areas in the country to take part in the project. A small 'Christian Science' group in Andover considered 'mass medication' to be fundamentally obnoxious and began a campaign against it. When fluoridation began on 17 July 1956 further protests occurred. An Anti-Fluoridation Association was set up and a few members of the Council who had originally voted in its favour now took up their cause. At the next elections in May 1957, four members of the Anti-Fluoride Independents were elected to the Council. The prime target of the AFA was the chairman of the Public Health Committee and he suffered much verbal abuse. The Attorney General in January 1958 gave permission for an action against the Council and by April that year they agreed to cease fluoridation after a five-year trial. This was not enough for the campaigners and at the council elections in 1958 they put up candidates in all the four wards who ousted the standing chairmen of both Finance and Public Health.

132. *Andover High Street in 1953. The flags celebrate the Coronation of Elizabeth II, outside Parsons and Hart, Waterloo House. Woolworth's now occupies the site.*

As a result, on 1 November 1958 the Council voted to immediately stop fluoridation of the town's water supply.

FREEDOM FOR THE RAF

To mark respect for the work of the Royal Air Force in Andover the RAF was granted the Freedom of Entry to the Borough on 14 September 1955. This gave it the right to march through the streets of the Borough armed "with swords drawn, bayonets fixed, colours flying, drums beating and bands playing" and was the highest honour that Andover Borough could bestow. *(See illustrations 136 and 137.)*

THE END OF THE LINE

Traffic on the old M&SWJR railway gradually declined to the extent that British Railways reduced through traffic to one train daily each way between Cheltenham and Andover in 1958. On 9 September 1961 trains from Andover Ford Junction to Andover were withdrawn and the line from Ludgershall to Swindon was closed. It was the death knell for this local railway for according to British Rail it had been losing £113.000 a year. Just before closure as a final fling on August Bank Holiday 1961 a regular train, *Cookham Manor*, had to be increased to twelve coaches to cope with the traffic. The only remains of the M&SWJR are two short arms from Swindon and the branch from Andover to the MOD base at Ludgershall.

In October 1963 news came that Dr Beeching was recommending the closure of the Andover to Southampton line. The Corporation's efforts

133. *The Coronation bonfire built on the golf course off Old Winton Road, 1953.*

134. *Opening of Andover Carnival in 1953, by Michael Denison and Dulcie Gray, seated on each side of the mayor.*

135. A tug-of-war at the Coronation celebrations in 1953.

136. The RAF was granted Freedom of Entry to Andover in 1955. In the picture the mayor, Cllr Norris, and the Commanding Officer of RAF Andover, Wing Commander G.M. Wyatt, take the parade in the High Street.

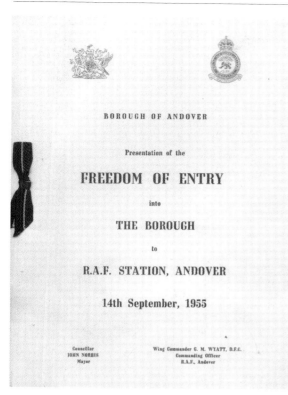

BOROUGH OF ANDOVER

Presentation of the

FREEDOM OF ENTRY

into

THE BOROUGH

to

R.A.F. STATION, ANDOVER

14th September, 1955

Councillor
JOHN NORRIS
Mayor

Wing Commander G. M. WYATT, D.F.C.
Commanding Officer
R.A.F., Andover

137. Souvenir programme for the occasion of the RAF being granted Freedom of Entry to Andover.

to retain it were in vain and the level-crossing gates of the Sprat and Winkle line closed for the last time in September 1967.

TOWN EXPANSION AND NEW BLOOD

In the post-war period the London County Council was urging manufacturing businesses to move out of London to undeveloped sites along main railway lines. In 1952 the government passed a Town Development Act, which gave the powers for an existing town to expand rather than build a completely new town as had happened at Harlow in Essex. The Hampshire County Council was approached by the LCC to agree to enlarge some of the towns on the main line from London to Exeter: Basingstoke and Andover were chosen.

At a meeting in the Drill Hall in 1961, there was much dissent over the siting of an 'overspill' town at Andover and an Anti-Overspill Committee was formed to oppose this on the Council. In contrast to the Anti-Fluoridation campaign, the new organisation was unsuccessful and the scheme was approved in May 1961.

The Plan allocated two areas, one at Walworth

138. A disastrous crash occurred on a September morning in 1961. The brakes of a lorry in Micheldever Road failed and it careered down London Street and crashed into four cars at the traffic lights outside the Foresters Arms. One woman died and four others were hurt.

on the east side, then but a few cottages, and at Portway on the west, on which factories and units could be built for companies wishing to transfer part or all of their business to a more attractive setting. As a consequence, the town centre was to be remodelled, providing new schools, and shops and satellite housing estates were to be built for the new population – 6,000 new homes were to be erected.

REMODELLING

From February 1968 through to the early 1970s the centre part of the town was extensively remodelled to create a modern shopping centre. This involved a considerable amount of demolition so that the Chantry Way shopping precinct

139. The signing of the Andover Town Development Scheme in May 1961, by the mayor, Cllr P.S. Batchelor.

140. Scott's shoe shop on the corner of the High Street behind the Guildhall in 1962, demolished to make way for the new Centre.

141. The opening of the Chantry Way Shopping Centre in October 1970.

and its associated car parking could be built. The first buildings under the bulldozer were in White Bear Yard allowing access to clearance work. In May 1968 Willis & Sons' shop in the High Street closed for business and it and the alley beside it, known as Fourthorp's Yard, disappeared. The mayor opened the first phase of the new Town Centre in October 1970 to huge crowds.

The second phase, finished in November 1970, comprised eleven shops underneath a new public library at first-floor level. The largest and most impressive of the old shops that were demolished was the former Scott's shoe shop. It was for about a hundred years the offices of Poore's Brewery, closing around 1920.

The new Town Centre and the open-air Chantry Way shopping centre were completed in 1971. Also new community facilities were provided at Cricklade College in Charlton Road, and there were new law courts and a sports centre next to the College.

Princess Alexandra opened the Andover Sports Centre at Cricklade in Charlton Road, on 5 November 1975. It contains a 25-metre main swimming pool, a teaching pool, a sauna and facilities for gymnastics, martial arts, badminton, squash, netball, archery and cricket.

The population of Andover was approximately 17,000 before the Town Development Plan but by 1971 it had risen to about 26,000 with a projection to reach 80,000 in the following ten years.

In the new estates on the edge of the town Floral Way was the first to be built (from 1964) and King Arthur's Way, Cricketers Way, River Way and Pilgrims Way soon followed. Each of the estates was landscaped with trees and shrubs planted imaginatively but by March 1965 the first complaints were heard of crumbling perimeter walls and poor standards of construction.

Balksbury County Primary School opened in September 1966 to serve the Floral Way Estate and took pupils from the then recently closed Norman Gate Primary School.

The first of the new firms to arrive in March 1965 was a printer, Collins and Wilson, which moved into the Walworth Industrial Estate;

142. *View from St Mary's church tower c.1964, looking down the Upper High Street.*

143. *The first tenants in the Town Development housing at Floral Way, September 1964, being welcomed by Cllr. Laurie Porter (left) and the mayor and mayoress.*

meanwhile work was progressing on John Laing's factory on the same estate. Robert Legg, makers of machinery for the tobacco industry, developed their new works in Newbury Road. Over the next few years diverse businesses moved in dealing in printing, publishing, engineering, tea and coffee blending, rubber products, cable guy ropes and cable end covers, motor cycle distribution, sanitary fittings, 'instant' houses, numbering machines, television cameras and mobile studios, container bodies for lorries, computer parts, aircraft staging, electronic devices and even billiard cues. Twinings, a name synonymous with tea and coffee, established by Thomas Twining in 1706, moved its headquarters to Andover in 1967, a town almost half way between the traditional tea ports of Bristol and London. Here they built a large modern factory.

DEVELOPMENT WOUND DOWN

As the 1970s waned so did the government's regional policies and the movement of jobs out of London was no longer encouraged. In 1980 the Town Development scheme was wound down as it became apparent that without new employers the housing programme could not be supported. By then just over 3, 200 homes had been built out of the 6,000 planned and the population was still only 27,000. Furthermore, complaints about the quality of the new developments still abounded and it was estimated that refurbishment would cost betweent £5 million and £20 million. The Greater London Council paid over a once-only sum of £14 million to pay for renovation.

Since then the Andover Area Draft Plan (1984) has increased growth and the population had reached 29,000 in 1991 and is expected in the new census to be around 39,500.

144.   *As part of the government's cutbacks in 1964, the wing section of the dismantled TSR2 supersonic jet winds its way through London Road, Andover, on 20 June 1967.*

A HOSPITAL SAVED

Just as the town was expanding in 1966 the Wessex Regional Hospital proposed to close Andover Hospital except for a geriatric department. All other facilities were to be transferred to district hospitals in Winchester and Basingstoke, leaving Andover residents to travel a minimum of fourteen miles. A 'Save the Andover Hospital Committee' was formed, calling upon local councils to help fight the proposal. Unusually, the councils acted in unison and a deputation of councillors, doctors and clergy led by Dr Ivor Jeffery-Machin went to Parliament to lobby to keep the hospital open. They succeeded, and if it were not for them we would not have a hospital today.

THE TROGGS

In the 1960s when the rest of the country's teenagers were dancing and singing along to the music of Cliff Richard and The Shadows, The Kinks, The Who etc., Andover had its own group. The Troggs were made up of Reg Ball (who later

145.   *The Country Bumpkin Club, an early performing home for The Troggs, seen here in the late 1960s.*

146. The Troggs in 2000.

changed his name to Reg Presley) fronting the band, Chris Britton on lead guitar, Ronnie Bullins and Staples. The band was a great hit with the locals, playing at the old Drill Hall, then refurbished into a discothèque and renamed The Country Bumpkin Club, and began to get themselves known nationally. In 1966 they were signed by Larry Page, manager of The Kinks, and to CBS records for their first single, *Lost Girl*. Their most famous song, *Wild Thing*, got to no 2 in the charts, and *With a Girl Like You* they got to no. 1.

The band broke up with Britton and Staples leaving, while Presley went on to pursue a solo career. In the late 1980s the Troggs reformed and are again a major live performing act, still boasting two founder members, with Presley again fronting the band and Chris Britton on lead guitar. They were joined by Peter Lucas on bass guitar and Dave Maggs on drums. In 1992 The Troggs collaborated with members of another group, REM, who are lifelong Troggs fans, resulting in an album entitled *Athens Andover*, which links the home towns of the two bands in the US and UK. In May 1994, another pop group, Wet Wet Wet, released the Presley favourite *Love is All Around*. The song was used in the successful film *Four Weddings and a Funeral* and became the biggest selling single of 1994, topping the charts for 15 weeks.

NEW ROADS

Northern Way was opened to traffic on 12 June 1968 to provide a link from the Folly Inn, Charlton Road to New Street across the marshlands, and immediately eased the traffic flow through the town centre. It took ten months to complete and was the first stage of a £500,000 scheme to improve the internal road system of Andover. The second stage joined the Folly roundabout to Bridge Street and followed the line of the old town railway.

The old A303 route through the town included the previous turnpike road (Micheldever Road), London Street, Bridge Street, Western Road and Weyhill Road. As the town expanded this route became very congested and even though the level-crossing gates in Bridge Street, scene of many hold-ups through the '50s and '60s, were now permanently open, this was little relief.

An Andover bypass opened in 1969, taking traffic around the town from Cow Down to 100-Acre Corner at the top of Weyhill Road, this becoming the main London-Exeter route A303. At that time the road passed through Weyhill and Mullenspond and it was not until after the closure of Andover airfield in 1977 that the road was once again altered from 100-Acre Corner to Mullenspond, cutting across a large corner of the old airfield.

147. Construction of the Andover bypass in 1970.

CLOSING DOWN

The Quarter Sessions, which have been held in the town since the granting of the the town's charter in 1599, came to an end on 14 December 1971 with a small ceremony, after which they were removed to Winchester. The Magistrates' Court however continued at the Guildhall until the new Court House was built within the Cricklade complex and opened in 1976. Also in the 1970s the farmers' Corn Exchange, held on the forecourt and ground floor of the Guildhall for over 150 years, ceased.

THE END OF LOCAL POWER

Under the Local Government Act of 1972 Andover Borough Council and Andover Rural District Council were amalgamated with Romsey and Stockbridge Rural District Councils to become Test Valley District Council. The inaugural meeting of the new authority was held in Andover Guildhall on 21 June 1973. On its formation, Andover's town symbols, mayor and even its heritage seemed to be lost and so an organisation, based on the town wards, was set up called the Andover Charter Trustees, managed by the town councillors. These upheld the powers vested in the Andover charters, looked after the extensive town archive and had the power to elect their own town mayor.

In the early months of 1976 Test Valley District Council petitioned the Queen to grant it Borough status. This was opposed by a great number of the town's councillors, Charter Trustees and inhabitants. A counter-petition containing over 4,000 names was forwarded to the Queen. The petitioners even obtained the services of a barrister to fight their cause, but after a long period of deliberation the Privy Council advised her Majesty to sign the District Council's request.

148.   A reminder of Andover's past. The corn market was held each Friday until the late 1960s on the forecourt of the Guildhall. This photograph was taken in 1860, and could well be the earliest known photograph taken in the town. It also features the offices of Barker, Son and Isherwood in the background.

149. Andover Guildhall and market in the late 1960s. The Guildhall was the centre of local government for 800 years.

This action deprived Andover of the right of any form of self-government and management of its own affairs, a privilege it had held for over 800 years. The office of mayor was extinguished at noon on 9 December 1976; its last incumbent was Cllr F.C.P. (Peter) Sumner. With the new charter came the power to elect a Test Valley Borough Mayor and to maintain and look after the existing heritage of the town and district. Today the Andover Town maces, civic regalia and charters are in the care of the Council and reside in Andover Museum in Church Close.

The new Borough Council set up its headquarters at Beech Hurst in Weyhill Road – previously the headquarters of the Andover Borough Council – with another important office at Duttons Road in Romsey. Soon the old Beech Hurst mansion was too small and in 1989, Hall and Tawse, the Southampton based contractors for

TVBC, demolished the old house and replaced it with a £6.33 million headquarters, paid for by selling off surplus Council property. The new building, constructed around a central courtyard, is in a mock-Tudor style. It was operating fully by June 1991.

The new Borough Council to its credit commissioned a market research team in June 1987 to determine the strength of feeling in the town for a parish or neighbourhood council, and a working party was set up to see how other towns in the country had managed since the 1972 Act. The unfortunate wording in a proposal document led to only six local councillors voting for the proposals and the motion was lost. Andoverians have today resigned themselves to the new regime and the Test Valley Borough Council is working hard to provide the town with facilities appropriate to the 21st century.

150. The Borough of Andover's coat-of-arms, granted to it in 1949. The eagle represents the town's long association with the RAF.

152. The coat-of-arms of Test Valley Borough Council.

THE TEST VALLEY TAPESTRY

The loss of Andover's civic identity was felt badly. Councillors argued that Romsey and Andover had little in common. Something needed to be done to pull the two units together and Laurie Porter, former mayor of Andover and mayor of Test Valley in 1983, came up with the idea that the natural beauty and varied history of the new Borough could be pulled together by societies and organisations in all the towns and parishes working on a joint project.

He proposed what is known as the 'Test Valley Tapestry', an embroidered set of views of the

151. The Andover panel from the Test Valley Tapestry.

various parts of the new authority. Fifty-five villages and three towns were encouraged to take part in the project over a six-year period – Porter himself did much of the work. The Tapestry was funded by the Borough's Lottery Fund, had its first showing at an exhibition in Andover Museum in 1990, and after being displayed at exhibitions in Stockbridge Town Hall and in Romsey Abbey it now resides in Test Valley Council's offices in Beech Hurst.

A DIFFERENT TOWN EMERGING

Over the years Andover's links with its weaving history have been eroded and Stretch Acre and Mud Town have long gone, save for a few houses in Recreation Road. In April 1974 most of Rack Close, formerly known as Lardicake Lane was demolished together with what was once The Wheatsheaf, a nineteenth-century beerhouse. The name Rack Close survives and describes the manner in which cloths were put on 'tenterhooks' to stretch them, but now most of the houses are gone, with the exception of a small row behind East Street between the United Reform Church and the Borough Arms public house.

The demolition of a row of houses on the north side of London Street, from just opposite the Kings Head public house to the junction with the old East Street, began in 1975. Two years later further demolition took place on the same side from the junction with East Street and London Road, up as far as the fire station. From September 1976 Hampshire County Council began demolition in Winchester Street including the Masons Arms public house to make way for a new southern distributor road linking Winchester Street with the town centre.

The Baptist church, which had stood in the High Street from 1866, was taken down after completion of a new church in Charlton Road in 1981. Dixon's electrical shop now stands on the site of the old church. The Walled Meadow, the former home of the Andover Football Club, was sold in 1982 for £2,121,800 for housing; the club moved into a new stadium at Portway Industrial Estate.

A hostel for homeless families known as Eastfield Lodge was completed in 1991 in the grounds of Eastfield House, in London Road. It provides ten small flats and is used for temporary housing. The former Rural District Council offices in Junction Road are now used for a similar purpose.

Twenty years after the opening of the Chantry Way shopping precinct it was considered a little

153. *Andover's latest character – the 'Town Crier'. He is seen on market day up and down the High Street (photo 2001).*

dated and unsuited to the needs of the expanding town. The joint owners of the site, Test Valley BC and Sun Life Assurance put forward a bold plan to roof over the existing precinct, giving a more comfortable environment. They were to provide new shop units by closing off pedestrian access to the precinct via West Street and building into the surface car park. A new 650-space, multi-storey car park was to replace the existing 400-car space surface park, and linking that to the centre would be a new shopping area with space for a large store. At that time there was a proposal for a new hotel, incorporating Ford Cottage, a sixteenth-century farm building, at the corner of Chantry Street and West Street. Unfortunately the hotel scheme did not come to fruition and the old cottage lies rotting behind advertising hoardings.

The new £10 million Chantry Centre opened during Easter 1990. It is modern and airy with a central courtyard that has replaced a rather drab area. From the deal the town has benefited from a new bus station and taxi rank and some shops have even been encouraged back from out-of-town sites.

Bibliography

Introduction
The Buildings of England – Hampshire and the Isle of Wight, by Nikolaus Pevsner and David Lloyd (1967).

The Environs of Andover
Andover: the Archaeological Implications of Development (Andover District Excavation Committee, 1973).
A parochial history of St Mary Bourne, by Joseph Stevens (1888).
Shell Guide to reading the landscape, by Richard Muir (1981).
A History of Hampshire, by T.W. Shore (1892).
Wessex before the Celts, by J.F.S. Stone (1958).
An Introduction to Field Archaeology as illustrated by Hampshire, by J.P. Williams-Freeman (1915).
Collins Field Guide to Archaeology in Britain, by E.S. Wood (1967).
The Test Valley Official Guide (1988).
A School History of Hampshire, by F. Clarke (1909).
Andover, the last 4000 years, by Dacre and Earney (Cricklade College, Andover, 1975).
Early Britain, by Jacquetta Hawkes (1987).

Romans, Saxons and Vikings
Danebury: anatomy of an Iron Age hillfort, by Barry Cunliffe (1974).
Danebury: an Iron Age hillfort in Hampshire, by R. Palmer (1984).
An introduction to Celtic coins, by Derek Allen (1978).
The Roman invasion of Britain, by Graham Webster (1980).
Andover, the last 4000 years (as above).
Hampshire Nunneries, by Diana Coldicott (1989).
Highways and Byways in Hampshire, by D.H. Moutray Read (1908).
A History of Hampshire (see above).
A School History of Hampshire (see above).
The Warrior Kings of Saxon England, by Ralph Whitlock (Moonraker Press 1977).
'The Saxons in Andover', by Max Dacre in *Test Valley Archaeological Committee Review* (1979).
Beyond the Old Royal Road, by Gordon Lee (Wodeland Publications, 1941).
History of the Kings of England by William of Malmesbury, ed. J. Stevenson.
Southampton through the ages, by Elsie M. Sandell (1976).
From Alfred to Henry III, 871-1272, by Christopher Brooke (1961).
In Search of the Dark Ages, by Michael Wood (1981).
The Anglo-Saxon Chronicle, translated by G.N. Garmonsway (1953).
Hampshire Notes and Queries Vol. V, p125.
History of Andover, by Elizabeth Mathews (Andover Public Library 1971).
Notes on the parishes of Fyfield, Kimpton, Penton Mewsey, Weyhill and Wherwell, by Rev. R.H. Clutterbuck (1898).
'Excavations at Old Down Farm', by S.M. Davies in *Hampshire Field Club Proceedings*, vol. 37, 1981).

Roads and Tracks of Britain, by Christopher Taylor (1979).
An etymological schedule of place names in the Andover district, by Edmund Parsons (c.1925).
'The excavation of nine Romano-British burials at Andover, Hampshire in 1984 and 1987', by Karen Jennings in *Hampshire Studies 2000, Proceedings of the Hampshire Field Club and Archaeological Society* vol. 55.

Domesday and Beyond
The Anglo-Saxon Chronicle (see above).
Domesday Book – Hampshire, ed. by Julian Munby (1982).
The Royal Forests of England, by J. Charles Cox (1905).
History of Hampshire (as above).
The Andover Woollen Industry, by Edmund Parsons (H.M. Gilbert, 1946).

Tudor Times
Andover in Hampshire: Life in the town before 1720, by Melville T.H. Child (1969).
The Martyrs of Hampshire, by the Rt Rev. Mgr J.H. King (Catholic Truth Society, 1935).
'Men of Andevor', *Andover Records* 6, by H.W. Earney

Plague, Scandal and Civil War
Acts of the Privy Council 1601-4, p211
The Civil War and Interregnum, by Anthony C. Raper (Andover Local History and Archaeological Scy 1994).
Cromwell, our Chief of Men, by Antonia Fraser (1973).
The Civil War in Hampshire, by G.N. Godwin (1904).
Weyhill Fair, by Anthony C. Raper (1988).

Interregnum and Restoration
Historical memorials of a Christian Fellowship, by J.S. Pearsall.
Don Quixot Redivivus Encountering a Barns Door (contemporary discourse on the New Street Barn case).
The Civil War and Interregnum (as above).

The Eighteenth Century
Discovering the Westward Stage, by Margaret Baker, Jack Gould and Eric Rayner (1972).
'A Carpenter's Contract', in *Test Valley and Border Anthology* No. 1 (Andover Local Archives Committee, 1973).
The Community of Andover before 1825, by Melville T.H. Child (Andover Local Archives Committee, 1972).
Through the doors of Andover Guildhall, by Anthony C. Raper (Test Valley Borough Council. 1981).
The Story of Savoy Chambers, Andover, ed. Victor Emery (Crest Estates 1982).
'The Heaths of Andover', by Anthony C. Raper in *Test Valley and Border Anthology* no. 10 (Andover Local Archives Committee, 1976).
'Men of Andevor' (as above).
'Inns of Andover', by H.W. Earney (*The Amateur Winemaker*, 1971).
A History of the Andover Grammar School, by Bennett and Parsons (1920).
'The Wakeford family and their bank in the 18th century', by Diana K. Coldicott, in *Lookback at Andover* (Andover History and Archaeology Society, 1993).

'Andover Old Bank and its failure in 1826', by Diana K. Coldicott, in *Lookback at Andover* (Andover History and Archaeology Society, 1994).
'The Token Coinage of Andover', by Anthony C. Raper, in *Test Valley and Border Anthology* no. 7 (Andover Local Archives Committee, 1975).
Directory of Hampshire (Pigot 1830).
Information from a handwritten note by Melville Child.
The Thomas Racket Papers 17th-19th centuries, ed. H.S.L. Dewar (Dorset Record Society, 1965).

The Iron Man of Andover
The poor blacksmith made rich, by the Rev. Richard Knill.
Waterloo Iron Works, by L.T.C. Rolt (1969).
'Quicksilver', a hundred years of coaching, by R.C. & J.M. Anderson.
Discovering the Westward Stage (as above).
Farms, Fairs and Felonies, by Melville T.H. Child (1967).
A History of the Andover Grammar School (see above).
Highways and Byways in Hampshire (see above).
The story of St Mary's parish church, Andover, by Arthur C. Bennett (St Mary's, Restoration Appeal).

The Scandal of Andover Workhouse
The Scandal of Andover Workhouse, by Ian Anstruther (1973).
The Red Guide – Hampshire, by Barry Shurlock (1989).
The Village Labourer, by J.L. & B. Hammond (1911).
English Social History, by G.M. Trevelyan (1948).
Poor Law in Hampshire through the centuries, a guide to the records (Hampshire Archivists' Group, 1970).

The Arrival of Railways
History, Gazetteer and Directory of Hampshire and the Isle of Wight 1859.
Catalogue of the papers of Lord [William] George Cavendish Bentinck.
A record of discussion at 'Memories Meeting', (Andover History Group 1951).
Battlebags, by Ces Mowthorpe.
Andover and the Elementary Education Act of 1870, by Janet Raper. (Dissertation for Graduate Certificate in Education, University of Newcastle-upon-Tyne 1975-76).
Inns of Andover (see above).
Andover Advertiser information ex Derek Tempero.
'Men of Andevor' (as above).

Fire and Riot
Andover Town Trail, a walkabout guide to the town by H.W. Earney and A.C. Raper (Andover Local History Society 1983 and 1988).

A record of discussion at 'Memories Meeting' (as above).
'The Andover riots of 1914', by David Borrett, in *Lookback at Andover* Vol. 1 No. 10.
'Electricity comes to Andover', by Erica Tinsley, in *Lookback at Andover* 1991.

Wings over Andover *and* War and Peace
Bomber Squadrons of the RAF and their aircraft, by Philip Moyes (1964).
'Wings over Andover', by Anthony C. Raper, in *Andover Digest* magazine, June/July 1986.
The Bruneval Raid, by George Millar (1984).
Daily Express, 23 April 1919.
ABC of the RAF, ed. by Sir John Hammerton.
Customs and traditions of the Royal Air Force, by Squadron Leader P.G. Hering (1961).
Andover at War, by Derek J. Tempero (Andover Local History Society and Hampshire Museum Service, 1984).
A history of the Hurstbourne and Fullerton Railway, by Ed. Goodridge (1985).
Amport, the story of a Hampshire parish, by Marigold Routh (1986).
Hampshire airfields in the Second World War, by Robin J. Brooks (1996).
Hampshire Industrial Archaeology, a guide, ed. Monica Ellis (Southampton University Industrial Archaeology Group 1975).
The Hants County Book, ed. S.C. Kendall (1938).

New Blood
Andover, an historical portrait, by J.E.H. Spaul (Andover Local Archives Committee, 1977).
Andover, a pictorial history, by Derek J. Tempero (1991).
The story of Andover Baptist Church 1824-1974, by Dr Barrington White and the Rev. Walter Fancutt (1974).
Andover Area Local Plan, Test Valley Borough Council (1984).
Andover, a town with a future, Andover Town Development Joint Committee (1972).
'Andover: 800 years of corporate life comes to an end', by Clive Burton in *Hampshire Mgazine*, Aug 1977.

General
The files of the *Andover Advertiser* and the *Southern Evening Echo*.

INDEX
An asterisk denotes a picture or caption

Á COURT, Col. C.A. 79, 80
Abbotts Ann 16, 18, 63, 79
Admiral's Way estate 15
Agricultural Riots 67, 69
Airship 102, *103
Aldred, Thomas 28
Alexandra, Princess 131
Alfred, King 19
Alphege, Bishop of Winchester 21
AMOCO UK 12
Amport 22, 79
Amport House 114, *116
Andover: administration 25-26, 33-34, 124, 136-137; chain of office 94; charters 25-26, 33-34; coat-of-arms *138; fires 25, 29, 41, 56-57, 98, *100, *101, 102, 109, 112; geology 9, *10; Members of Parliament 28, 35, 37-38, 43, 49, 50, 52, 66, 83, *105; origin of name 16; population 131, 133; weights and measures *61
Andover, Battle of 40-41, *40
Andover Advertiser 84, 85-86, 92, 94, 118
Andover Aerodrome 13, 113-116, *113, *114, *115, 121, 135
Andover Archaeological Society 13, 15, 17, 18
Andover Brewery *96, *97, 131
Andover bypass 135, *135
Andover Carnival *125, *127
Andover Chamber of Commerce 109
Andover Co-operative Society 98, *99
Andover Cottage Hospital 84, *84, 134
Andover Down 87
Andover Football Club 92, *93, 139
Andover Forest 26
Andover Gasworks 60
Andover Grammar School 33, *33, 56, 63
Andover Guild of Merchants see Merchant Guild
Andover Junction station *91
Andover Lighting and Power Co. 72
Andover Loyal Volunteers 56
Andover Market 26, 30, 34, 120, *137
Andover Museum 15, 122, 137
Andover Nosegay 85, *86
Andover Old Bank 60, *62
Andover Postboy *75
Andover Power Station 107, *107
Andover Road station 89, *90

Andover Round Table 125
Andover Sports Centre 131
Andover Standard 86, *86
Andover Temperance Society 77
Andover Theatre *59, 60
Andover Trades Council 109
Andover Union 79
Andover Volunteer Fire Brigade 94
Andover Yeomanry Cavalry 69-70, *70
Andover-Redbridge Canal *54, 54-55, *55, 58, 77, 78, 89
Angel Inn 29-30, *30, 53, 60, 94
Anna Valley 102
Annett & Son 84
Anti-fluoridation 125-126
Anti-Overspill Committee 129
Anton Mill 23
Anton river 12, 16, *99
Appleshaw 18, 79
Archaeological finds 10-16, *10, *11, *12, *16, 17-19
Archer, Fred 88
Archery 28-29
Armstead, Alderman W.J. 118, *118
Aspin, R. 98
Atkins, Elizabeth 55
Aubertin, Charles 57
Ayton, Brassey, Lee & Salterthwaite 60, 62

BADDEBY, John 26
Baker, Dorothy 49
Baker, Mr 80
Baker, Robert 65
Balksbury 11, 13, 14
Balksbury County Primary School 131
Ball's Cottages 98
Banking 57, 60, 62
Banks, Alexander 49
Banks, T.A. *87
Baptists 139
Barnard, Phillip 44
Barton Stacey 79, 117, 118
Basingstoke 9, 89
Batchelor's barn 96
Beale, Frank 95, *104
Beare, Mr 50
Beck, Gabriel 43
Beckingham, Phyllis 102-104
Beech Hurst, Weyhill Road 124, 137, 139
Belcher, Tom 67
Benefactions Tablet 28, *29, 48
Bensley, John Benjamin 67
Bensley, Thomas jnr and snr 67
Bentinck, Lord George 87
Bere Hill *8, 12, 89
Beta airship 102, *103
Bibury Club 87, 88
Billing, Joseph 67
Bishops Court House *54, *90, 96
Blacksmiths Arms 98, 102
Blagdon Copse 14

Blake, Peter 43
Blake, Richard 48
Blake, William 38, 39
Blendon Drive 15
Bloxham, P. 102
Body, John 31
Bowles, Mr 60
Bowling Green House see Folly Inn
Braishfield 11
Brassey, Thomas 89
Brassey, Lee & Son 60
Brewing 53, 57-58
Brick-kiln Street 66
Bridge Street 36, 54, *54, 73, 75, 96, *97, 98, *98, 103, 107, 118, 120, 135
British Red Cross Society 117, 118
Browne, Frederick 86
Bull, William 78
Bullington 79
Bury Hill 13, 14, *14, 22
Bush Inn, Bridge Street 54
Butcher, Richard 44

CALVERT, Bernard 36-37
Cannon, Tom 87, 88, *89
Carr, William 41
Catherine Wheel coffee house 98
Celebrations: marriage of Duke and Duchess of York 1893 *99; peace after 1st World War 106, *106; silver jubilee George V 112, *112; peace after 2nd World War 123, *124; coronation Elizabeth II 125, *126, *127, *128;
Central Club *117
Chantry Street 11, 68, 139
Chantry Way shopping precinct 130-131, *131, 139
Chapel River Press 109
Charles I, King 37, 39, 40-41
Charlton 11, 19
Charlton, Alderman R. 124
Charlton Road 104, 131
Chaucer Avenue 15
Chauncy, Dr Isaac 44
Chestnuts, The, Bridge Street 96
Chilbolton 10, 11, 79
Chit, Roger 27
Church Close 15, 137
Chute 79
Chute Forest 26, 79
Civil Defence 117, *117, 118, *118, 119, *119, *120, 121, *121, *123
Civil disturbance 102-104
Civil War 37-42
Clanville 42, 79
Clare House, East Street *117, 118
Clarendon Park 40, 43
Clark, Rev. Robert 38-39
Clarke, Charles 84-85, *85
Clarke, W. Percival 103, 109

Clatford 43
Cleave Hill 17
Cloth production *27, 28, *51, 139
Clutterbuck, Rev. 22
Cnut, King 21-22, *22
Coaches 53-54
Cobbett, William 67, 69, 79
Coke Hole Trust 84
College Inn 29
Colling & Tilling, bicycles 96
Collins & Wilson 131
Colt-Hoare, Sir Richard 18
Common Acre 28
Compton, T.H., corn and coal merchant 96
Congregationalists 65
Cook's Farm 98
Cooper, William 38
Corn Exchange 50, 136, *136
Country Bumpkin Club *134, 135
Cox, Bethel 69
Crang, M.J.T. *119
Cribb, Tom 67
Cricketers Way 131
Cricklade College 131
Cricklade manor 62
Cricklade Mill 23
Crimes 37, 65
Cromwell, Oliver 42
Croye Close 106, *106
Cunliffe, Prof. Barry 14

DACRE, Max and Peggy 13, *13, 15, 18
Dance family 96
Danebury 11, 13, 14-15, *15, *16, 17
Danebury Hotel (*previously White Hart Inn and Star and Garter*) 41, 53, 63 Danish Dock 19-20, *20
Davies R. 17
Davies, Sue 13
Day, John 87
Day, John Barnham 87
De Evinley, Hugh 28
De Morgan, Faith 11
Delaval, Sir Francis Blake 50
Denison, Michael 125, *127
Devereux, Robert 2nd Earl of Essex 33
Dixon, Dr 47
Dixon, Henry 42
Dixon's electrical shop 139
Dodson, Rev. Christopher 79, 83
Doles Wood 26
Domesday Survey 23
Drake, William 45
Drill Hall 105, 125, 129
Drouett, Jean 55
Dudley, Robert, Earl of Leicester 31, 35, *35

EAST CHOLDERTON 46
East Street 65, 68, 77, 94, *117, 139

East Tytherley 62
Eastern Avenue 18
Eastfield Cottages 68
Eastfield House 68, 139
Eastfield Lodge 139
Eastfield Road *51, 68, *68
Edgar, King 20, 21
Edward III, King 26
Edward VII, King (as Prince of Wales) 88
Edward VIII, King (as Prince of Wales) *114, 115
Electricity supplies 107, *107
Elizabeth, Queen (queen of George VI) 118, *118
Elizabeth I, Queen 33
Ellen, Frederick 58
Emigration to America 37
Ethelred II, King 19, 21, 22
Etwall, Ralph 83
Etwall, William 87
Etwall House 112
Evacuees 118-119
Ewelme Hospital 44-47, *45

FABER, Capt. Walter *105
Faccombe 11, 79
Fairfax, Sir Thomas 42, *42, 43
Fairs 34 (*see also Weyhill cattle and sheep fair and Weyhill cheese fair*)
Festing, Capt. Henry 63
Fiander, Henry 109
Figsbury 14
Finkley Down 12, 18
Finkley Forest 26
Fire fighting and fire brigades 94, 103
Fires *see* Andover: fires
First World War 105
Floral Way 131
Floyd, Gabriel 41
Fluen, Mary *125
Folly Inn (*previously Bowling Green House*) 56
Ford Cottage 139
Foresters' Hall, London Street 98
Forests 26
Forkbeard, Sweyn 21
Fourthorp's Yard 131
Fowle, George 65
Fowle, Martha 63
Fox, John Russell 86
Foxcotte 19, 79
Foxcotte chapel 23-24, 77
Franklin, William 42
Freeman, Dr Williams 13, 19
Freemantle Park 26
French prisoners and refugees in Andover 55, 56, 57, 68
Fyfield 79

GADBURY, Mary 42
Gale, Henrietta 77
Galliker Way 89
Gardiner, Major Charles 79
Gas supplies 72
Gates, veterinary surgeon 96

Gawler, Henry 79
Geology *see* Andover: geology
George Inn 52, 54, 69, *70, 72, 75
Gibbs, William 50
Gifford, Major 41
Gilbert, R.M. *119
Gilbert & Co. bank 57, 58
Gill, Robert 80
Goddard, Revd William S. 77, 78
Good, William 29
Goodworth Clatford 79
Gough, Robert 43
Grateley 13, 79
Gray, Dulcie 125, *127
Great Western Railway 77, 85
Green, Rev. Henry 80
Green, Samuel 82
Greenly, Rev. John 63
Gue, William 84, 94
Guild of Merchants *see* Merchant Guild
Guildhall 30, 33, 35, 49-50, *50, 136, *137

HAMILTON, Lady 63
Hampshire Archaeological Society 13
Hampshire Banking Co. 58
Hampshire County Council 129, 139
Hanson, John 33
Hanson, Katherine 28
Harrow Way 12, 27
Harvey, Vivian R. 102-104
Hawley, William H.T. 80, 81, 82
Hayward, William 48
Heath family 57-58, *58, 60
Heath & Co. bank 57, 58
Heath House 58
Henry VIII, King 28
Henry, Bishop of Winchester 24
Herbert family 96
Herberts, William 50
Hermit Lodge, Houghton Road 88
High Street 30, *32, 41, 54, 65, 69, 85, 87, 94, 103, 104, 107, *111, 120, *126, *130, 131, *132, *139
High View Farm, Kimpton 16
Highclere 47
Holmes, James Charles 86
Home Guard *see* Civil Defence
Horse racing 87-88, *88
Hundred Acres Farm 13
Hunt, Henry 69
Hunt, Solomon 44
Hurstbourne 10
Hurstbourne Tarrant 11, 14, 79

IN AND OUT Hundreds 26, 29, 34
Interregnum 43
Iremonger, Lascelles 69
Ironside, Edmund 22

JEFFERY-MACHIN, Dr Ivor 134
Jervis, William 38

John Lewis Partnership 12
John, King 25-26
Joyce, Hannah 82
Junction Hotel 104

KATHERINE WHEEL public house 75
Kelly's Directories 109, 114
Kempthorne, Sampson 80
Kimmer Farm 11
Kimpton 13, 16, 79
King Arthur's Way 131
King, J. 85
King, Young 87
King's Enham 21
Kingsclere 9, 26
Kingsclere, Battle of 70
Kingsmill, Sir George 36
Kingsmill, Sir William 31
Knights Enham 15, 28, 79
Knights Enham Hill 18
Knights Hospitaller 28
Konig, Fredrich 67

LADIES' Walk 89
Lamb, Thomas 79
Langdon, John Harris 50
Langtry, Lillie 88
Lansley, William 50
Lardicake Lane 139
Law courts 34, 35, 136
Le Riche, Alexander 28
Leckford 12
Lee family 60
Legg, Robert 133
Levellers 42
Linkenholt 79
Little Park 102, *103
Livesey, Augustus 77, 78
Lock, James 56
London & South Western Railway 11, *11, 84, 89
London County Council 129
London Lane *see* Vigo Road
London Road 68, 87, *134, 139
London Street 18, 57-58, 60, 98, 102, 107, 112, 139
Longparish 79
Longstock 20, *20
Loxley, Mrs John 84
Ludgershall 79

MAGISTRATES' COURT 136
Mail coaches 36, 72, 73, *74
March's Cottages 98
Marchant Road *87
Market *see* Andover Market
Marks, John 41
Marlborough Street 68
Marsh, Henry 69
Masons Arms 139
Matilda (daughter of Henry I) 24-25
Matilda (queen of King Stephen) 25
McCorquodale Printers 109
McDougal, Colin 80-83
McDougall's flour mills 109
Mead Road 107

Merchant Guild 25-26, 27
Methodists 96, *98
Micheldever 89
Micheldever Road *129
Micheldever station 89, *90
Midland & South Western Junction Railway 126
Millett, Mr 39
Mills 23, *23
Mills, E.A. 98
Millway Road *87
Montfort Missionaries 106
Montgomery, Field Marshal 119
Monxton 41, 79
Moon, Billy 88
Moore, John 34
Moore Hall 112
Moore's Garage *54
Mooring, Robert 44
Mud Town 68, 139
Munday, Benjamin 49
Mundy, Hugh 82
Museum of the Iron Age 15
Musters 29

NATIONAL SCHOOL 77
Neat, Will 66-67
Nelson, Horatio 63, *63
Nether Wallop 87
New Street 13, 94, 98, *100, *101, 102, 104, 112
New Street Jazz Band 106
New Street School 94
New Town Scheme *87
Newbury Road 133
Newbury Street 60
Newspapers 85-87
Newtown Close *87
Nicholas, Judge 42
Nonconformists 43-44, *44
Norman Court Farm 11
Norman Gate Primary School 131
Norris, Cllr *128
Northeast Mr 80
Northern Way 135
Noyes, Peter 37
Noyes, Thomas 49
Nutbane 11

O'MALLEY, Mike 11
Oglander, Sir John 37
Old Down Farm 13-14, 19
Old Winton Road 112
Olympic Games 124, *124

PAGE, Harry 107
Pain, James 68
Parker, Henry W. 83
Paulet, Lady Isabella 50
Peddar, Revd William 56
Pelican Inn 66
Penruddock, Col. John 43
Penton Grafton 79
Penton Lodge 88
Penton Mewsey 12, 79
Perry, Richard R. 67
Pest House 53, 96
Petersfield 9

Pheasant Inn see Winterslow Hut
Phillhill Brook 16
Piggott, Lester 88
Pilgrims Way 131
Plague 36
Plantation Road *87
Poaching 65-66
Policing 72, *72, 103-104, 124
Pollen, Sir John 50, 69
Pond, Cllr 96
Poor, condition of 79, 94
Poor Law Reform Act 1834, 79
Poor relief 79
Poore & Sons *96, *97, 131
Pope, Marie 29-30
Pope, Richard 29
Porter, Cllr Borseberry 112
Porter, Laurie 138
Portsea Island Co-operative Society 98
Portway Industrial Estate 12, 18, 139
Postal services 36
Pressley, Sir Charles 84
Priory Lodge 60
Prize fighting 66-67, 87
Pye, Henry James 55

QUAKERS 43, 60
Quarley 11, 69, 79
Quarley Hill 14
Quarter Sessions 136
Queen Charlotte public house 87

RACK CLOSE *51, 139
Racket, Rev. Thomas 62
Railways 89-91, 126
Rainsford, Sir Henry 37
Ramridge Cottage, Weyhill 79
Ramridge manor 44
Ransom, George 68
Rawlins, Thomas 60
Recreation Road 139
Redon Way 18
Reeks, J. Compton *104
Richmond, Adam 27
Ridding, Revd Charles Henry 77, 78
River Way 131
Roads 17, 52-53, 135, *135
Robinson, John 36
Roe's garage 102
Roman Catholics 105-106, *105, *106
Roman Way estate 18
Romans in Andover area 17-18, *17, *18
Romsey 10, 35, 137, 138
Rooksbury Mill 23
Rothsay Hotel, Weyhill 105
Round House 52, *52
Royal Air Force 113-116, 126, *128, *129
Royal Flying Corps 113, *114
Royal hunting lodge 20

ST FLORENT, abbey of 23-24, 26, 28
St Hubert Road *87
St John of Jerusalem, Order of 28
St John the Baptist RC church *106
St John's Ambulance Brigade 117, 118
St John's House 27
St John's Lane 27
St Mary's parish church 24, *24, 25, *25, 28, 38-39, 44, 48, 55, 77, 78, *78, 85
St Mary's Mission Hall 94
Salisbury Road 107
Samborne, Julius 48
Sanderson, Dr Randall 36
Sarson 22
Savoy Chambers 58
Savoy cinema 18
Sawyer, Sir Robert 46, 47
Saxons in Andover area 18-22
Schools 33, *33, 56, 63, 77, 94, 131
Scott's shoe shop *111, *130
Second World War 114-116, 117-123, *117-123
Sedgley, Harriet 57
Seeley, Maj-Gen J.E.B. 107
Shepherds Spring 11, 12
Ship Money 37
Shipton 79
Shipton Bellinger 10
Shubrick, General 52
Silent Man beerhouse 94
Silkweavers' Arms 68, *68
Silkweavers Road estate 13
Silkweaving 68, *68, 69, *69
Slade, John 31
Smannell 107
Smith, Humphrey 43
Smith, Col. Sir John 39
Smith, Thomas Ashetton 50, 65-66, *66, 69-70, *70
Sopers Lane see West Street
South Tidworth 43
Southampton Arms 41
Southern Newspapers Group 87
Spine Road 15
Spring, Thomas 66-67, *67
Sprint, Samuel 43-44
Stable, John 55
Stacpole, Hugh 79
Stage coaches 53-54, 72, 73
Star and Garter (later the Danebury Hotel) 73, *75, *76, 87, *105
Star Inn see White Hart Hotel
Startin W. 17
Station Hotel 96
Steele, Edmund 66
Stephen, King 24, 25
Steven's Bakery 98
Stockbridge 9, 55
Stockbridge Races 87-88, *88
Street lighting 72, 107
Stretch Acre 139
Sumner, Cllr. F.C.P. 137
Sun Life Assurance 139
Sutton, Mr 69

Swimming pools 92, 95, *95, 112, *112
Swindon, Marlborough & Andover Railway 89, 91
Switzar, Thomas 49

TALBOT, Frederick *72
Talbot Walker, solicitors 96
Tangley 79
Tarrant, Thomas 68
Tasker family and iron business 50, 63, *63, *64, 65, *65, 77
Temperance 77
Territorial Army 105, 112
Test river 10, 16
Test Valley Archaeological Trust (formerly Committee) 12, 13-14, 18
Test Valley Borough Council 136-137, 139; coat-of-arms *138
Test Valley District Council 95, 136
Test Valley Tapestry 138-139, *138
Test Way Walk 77
Thorn, John and Eleanor 53
Thorne, Wellesley 98
Thornton, Mr 60
Three Choughs 36
Three Tuns 66
Thruxton 18, 79
Tidworth 65, 79
Tidworth Camp 91
Tinkers Hill (Finkley Down) 16
Tinkers Hill (Picket Piece) 12, 18
Town Crier *139
Town Development Plan 129-130, *130, 132,
Town House see Guildhall
Town Mills 23, *23, *99
Trade tokens 48, 60
Troggs, The 134-135, *135
Tryggvason, Olaf 21
Turner, James 66
Turner, Joseph 50
Turnpike roads 52, 89
Twining tea company 15, 133

UNITED REFORM CHURCH, East Street 65
Upper Clatford 11, 22, 41, 65, 79
Upper Mill Farm, Monxton 41

VENTHAM, Richard 44
Vergil, Polydore 22
Vernham's Dean 13, 43, 79
Vernon, Harry 37-38
Vicar – ejection of 38-39
Vicarage 77
Victoria Park 98
Vigo Road 13, 53, 68, *69, 96
Vigo Road recreation ground 28, *104, 112, 125
Vikings 19-20, *19, *20, 21
Volunteers 56, 69-70
von Blomberg, General 115, *115

WAINWRIGHT, Dr Geoffrey 11
Wakeford Bank 60, *62, 67
Wakeford family 60, *62, 67, 77
Wakley, Thomas 82
Walled Meadow 92, *93, 112, 118, 125, 139
Waller, Sir William 37-38, *38, 40-41, 43
Wallop 11
Wallop, Robert 37
Walters, William 49
Walworth Industrial Estate 12, 131
War memorial 107, *107, *108
Warham, Edward 48
Waterloo House, High Street 65
Waterloo Iron Works 65, *65
Waterman, Goody 42
Watery Lane 27
Watts, Dr Isaac 44
Weaving *27, 28, *51
Wellington, Duke of 70
West Street (formerly Sopers Lane) 139
Westcombe, Thomas 44
Weyhill 12, 19, 22, 35, 37, 70
Weyhill cattle and sheep fair 20, 26, 34, 44-48, *45, *46, 53, 58
Weyhill cheese fair *72
Weyhill Road *87, 107, 109, *110, *111, 115, 124
Wharf House *54
Wherwell 19, 69, 79
Wherwell nunnery 24, 25
White, Mr 84
White, Revd Henry 53
White Bear Yard 29
White Hart Hotel (previously the Star Inn) 42, 73, *76
White Hart Inn (later Danebury Hotel) 41
White Swan Inn 44
Whithed, Sir Henry 36
Whitworth, Robert 54
William I, King 23
Willis & Sons 131
Willis, Richard 49
Wimbleton, Joseph 48
Winchester 9, 24-25
Winchester, Bishops of 21, 24, 28
Winchester, Marquis of 105, 114, *116
Winchester College 28, 29, 41
Winchester Street 18, 96, 139
Windover, John 50
Windsor Road *124
Winterslow Hut (previously Pheasant Inn) 72, *74
Witan 21
Wolversdene Club 119
Wood Lane see Bridge Street
Wool trade 27-28, *27, *51, 60
Workhouse 49, 79-83, *80, *81, *83, 102
Wyght, John 26-27
Wynn, Sir Richard 37

YOUR MOVE estate agents *58